Y0-DJQ-524

TEACH YOURSELF TENNIS!

A tennis MAGAZINE BOOK

TEACH YOURSELF TENNIS!

Edited by Robert J. LaMarche

Published by Golf Digest/Tennis, Inc.
A New York Times Company,
495 Westport Avenue,
Norwalk, Connecticut 06856

Trade book distribution by
Simon & Schuster,
A Division of Gulf + Western Corporation,
New York, New York 10020

First Printing
ISBN: 0-914178-39-3
Library of Congress: 80-66688
Manufactured in the United
States of America
Cover and book design by Dorothy Geiser.
Typesetting by J&J Typesetters, Norwalk, Conn.

Printing and binding by
R. R. Donnelley & Sons

CREDITS:

ILLUSTRATION:
Illustrations on pages 26-30, 74 (bottom), 75
(bottom), 79, Dick Kohfield; 126 (left), 127 (left),
129 (left), 132 (right), 134 (left), 135 (left), 136-137,
138, 140 (top), 141 (bottom), 144 (top), 146, 148,
150 (bottom), 151 (bottom), Ed Vebell; 86-87,
102-103, 117-123, 126 (right), 127 (right), 128, 129
(right), 132 (left), 133, 134 (right), 135 (right), 139,
140 (bottom), 141 (top), 144 (bottom), 145, 147, 149,
150 (top), 151 (top), 152, Elmer Wexler.

PHOTOGRAPHY:
Photograph on page 113 by Todd Friedman, all other
photographs by Jim Britt, John Newcomb, Steve
Szurlej and Ed Vebell.

CONTENTS

STRATEGY   115

INTRODUCTION

Stan Smith:
the world's No. 1 player in 1972 and one of the great champions of the 1970's.

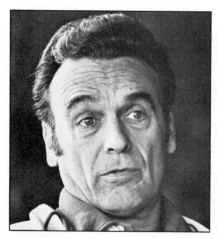

Vic Seixas:
an ex-Wimbledon and U.S. titlist who's one of the top seniors in the world.

Billie Jean King:
one of the game's greatest champions and most influential pioneers.

Julie Anthony:
a former high-ranked U.S. woman player who holds a Ph.D. in psychology.

Roy Emerson:
winner of more major singles championships (12) than any man in history.

Tony Trabert:
a former world champion and coach of the U.S. Davis Cup team.

Ron Holmberg:
a masterful touch player who ranked No. 4 in the U.S. a few years ago.

Imagine being surrounded at courtside by the likes of
Billie Jean King, Stan Smith, Tony Trabert, Roy Emerson,
Vic Seixas, Ron Holmberg and Julie Anthony—an awesome
assemblage of some of the greatest tennis minds in the world!
And what's more, they're all eager to assist you in your tennis
development, eager to share the vast wealth of tennis
knowledge that they've accumulated in their many years of
playing, coaching and teaching the game.

Just a wild dream? In actuality, perhaps. But these tennis
personalities *do* want to help you improve and get more
enjoyment out of the game. And the next best thing to actually
meeting and talking with them is to benefit from their expertise
in some other form of communication. That's precisely what
Teach Yourself Tennis! is all about.

The group of tennis stars mentioned above are all
members of the TENNIS magazine Instruction Advisory Board
and they've worked closely with the editorial staff of that
publication to bring you a book that lets you take charge of
your own tennis development, build a stronger game in
logical, easy-to-follow stages—and have a lot of fun doing it.
In fact, each chapter in **Teach Yourself Tennis!** gives you
the feeling that you're getting a private lesson from one of
the greats on the instruction panel.

Lavishly illustrated with hundreds of photographs, art
renderings and court diagrams, **Teach Yourself Tennis!** is
the end product of more than two years of hard work by
Advisory Board members and the editors of TENNIS. All of
the material in the book originally appeared in the magazine
as monthly installments of the widely-acclaimed
Instruction Portfolio series.

Best of all, **Teach Yourself Tennis!** is a very versatile
book. It has been structured carefully so that beginners can
use it to get started in tennis and progress steadily with each
chapter. But more than that, advanced players can use the
book both as a refresher course when shots go stale and to
develop previously untried strokes and strategies.

There are a lot of winners on the Instruction Advisory Board
who gave their time unselfishly to the production of the book,
and we think **Teach Yourself Tennis!** is a winner, too.
We hope you will agree.

—Robert J. LaMarche
Associate Editor
TENNIS magazine
August, 1980

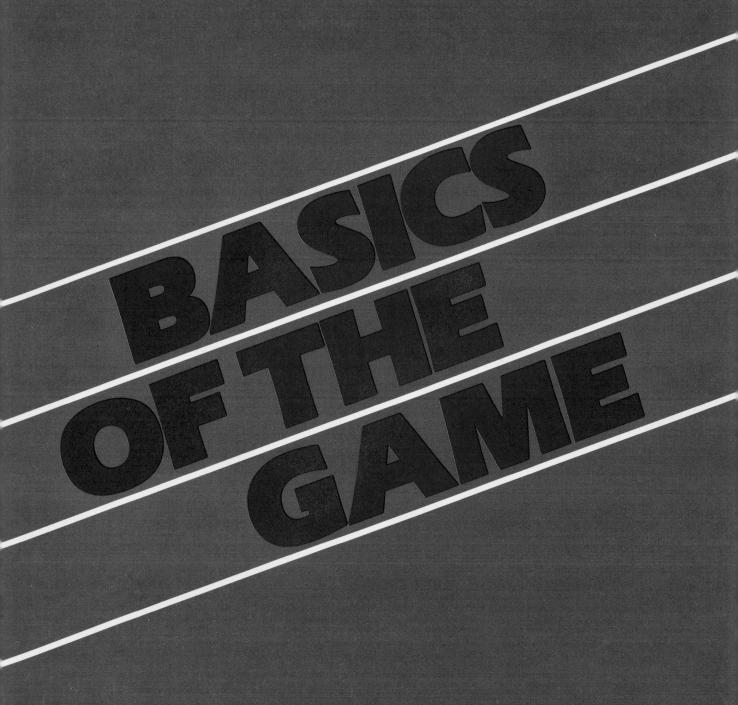

BASICS OF THE GAME

WHAT TENNIS IS ALL ABOUT

Tennis is a fast-moving, competitive racquet sport for either two players (called singles) or two pairs of players (doubles). It is played, either indoors or out, on a large playing area (the court) divided by a waist-high net. Simply stated, the idea of the game is to hit a ball with a racquet over a net in such a way that it bounces on your opponent's side of the court but yet cannot be effectively returned. Such a bold oversimplification, of course, hardly conveys the drama of a tennis match.

Much of the appeal of tennis lies in its competition. Since the opponents are separated by the net, their contest can be fierce yet civilized because physical contact should never occur. When that is combined with a scoring system (see next page) that may seem complex but is actually cleverly constructed to make winning rarely certain, a tennis match becomes an exciting confrontation that has many of the aspects of a duel.

Tennis, further, has considerable appeal at the physical level since merely hitting the ball and making it go where you intend calls for skills that require coordination, concentration and practice. A tennis player must also be able to anticipate the flight of the ball and move into position to hit it. That demands agility. And since a tennis match may last more than an hour, you need a certain stamina, too, to play consistently well.

But perhaps the most tantalizing aspect of the game is that complete mastery will always elude you. The better a player you become, the more challenging the game becomes. At times, tennis will leave you physically exhausted but mentally exhilarated. At other times, you may be depressed and frustrated.

Nonetheless, you will continue to work on your game, not merely to beat that opponent on the other side of the net, but to satisfy your own demands on yourself.

A THUMBNAIL HISTORY

The sport was devised in 1873 by an English country gentleman, Major Walter Clopton Wingfield, as an outdoor version of the ancient game of court tennis. Wingfield's creation caught on instantly and spread rapidly. But his original name for the game, "sphairistike," was quickly replaced by the term lawn tennis, which was more apt since the game was then played strictly on grass. It reached the U.S. in the spring of 1874 when the first lawn tennis court in this country was laid out on Staten Island, N.Y.

Tennis prospered as largely an upper-class diversion, in the process acquiring an effete image that took years to overcome. It attained early heights as a participant and spectator sport in the 1920's, thanks in part to the skills and charisma of such stars as Bill Tilden of the U.S. and Suzanne Lenglen of France. Lenglen, in fact, started the gradual trend to professionalism by getting $50,000 for a tour in 1926.

After World War II, tennis languished on both the participant and spectator levels. U.S. and Australian players dominated the tournament game and the premier team competition, the Davis Cup. But the sport suffered as its top male stars, such as Pancho Gonzalez and Rod Laver, turned professional and were ostracized by the tennis establishment. The big turning point for the game came in 1968 when open tennis was introduced, permitting the pros to enter the major tournaments that had previously been limited to amateurs.

With that, the tennis boom began. Spectator interest increased and so—perhaps coincidentally—did participant involvement, spurred by a new awareness of the benefits of vigorous leisure activity.

Today, with tennis' old elitist image a stereotype of the past, millions of Americans play the game regularly each week—many at the new indoor facilities that have made the game a year-round sport in even northern regions. Millions more watch, in person or on television, as a talented young generation of tennis stars compete for whopping tournament purses.

If golf was the sport of the immediate post-war years, then tennis is the sport of this era. What started out

as a delicate divertissement for ladies and gentlemen on the lawns of English country houses has emerged as a popular sport that can be enjoyed for a lifetime by almost anyone.

THE PLAYING AREA

A regulation tennis court measures 120 by 60 feet, although the playing area—the part in which the ball must bounce to stay in play—is 78 by 36 feet. Outdoor courts are usually surrounded by a wire fence to stop balls from going astray. Indoor courts have curtains that do the same thing.

The court surface may be asphalt, cement, clay (a loose but compacted granular material) or—very rarely these days—grass. Some modern courts are covered with a cushioned layer that's easy on the feet and many indoor courts use rubber or felt carpets over asphalt for the same reason.

SINGLES COMPETITION

In a singles match, the players spin a coin or a racquet to decide who will start the match—who will serve the first game. During each game, the server delivers the ball on alternate points into one of the opposite service boxes. He starts out on the right. He stands behind his baseline, just to the right of the center mark, lifts the ball in the air and hits it with an overhead swing so that the ball travels diagonally over the net and bounces inside his opponent's right-hand service box.

The server has two attempts to deliver a legal serve. If he fails to put the ball into the proper service court, that is called a fault; two failures are a double fault and the server loses the point. If a serve nicks the top of the net and lands in the proper service court, it's called a let and the server is awarded an extra serve.

The opponent—called the receiver when it is his turn to return serve—stands close to his baseline. If the ball is served correctly, he tries to get it back across the net so that it bounces within the server's full court; that is, inside the area bounded by the baseline and the singles sidelines.

The players then exchange shots, or rally, usually relying principally on

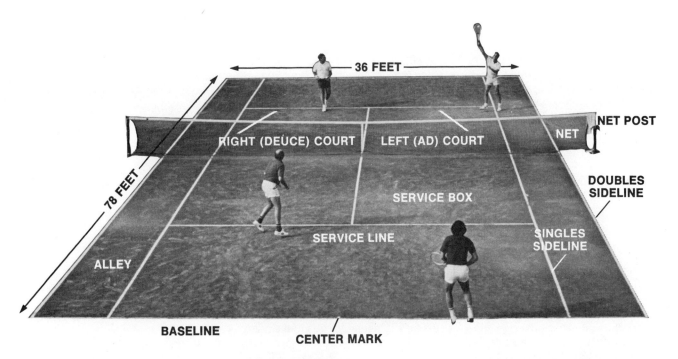

36 FEET

NET POST

RIGHT (DEUCE) COURT   LEFT (AD) COURT   NET

78 FEET

DOUBLES
SIDELINE

SERVICE BOX

SERVICE LINE

SINGLES
SIDELINE

ALLEY

BASELINE   CENTER MARK

the most basic shot, the ground stroke, which is meeting the ball after it has bounced once. A ground stroke is called a forehand, for a right-hander when the ball is hit on the right side of the body (left for left-handers), and a backhand when it's hit on the left side (right for left-handers).

Other key strokes are: the lob, which is a ball that's lofted high in the air; the volley, which is a ball that's hit on the fly before it bounces; the overhead smash, which is a ball that's met with an overhead swing similar to the serve; and the drop shot, which is a ball that falls just on the other side of the net.

Play continues on a point until it is lost—either when one player fails to return the ball before it bounces twice on his side of the net, when a player hits the ball so it lands outside the playing area or when a player hits the ball into the net.

Upon completion of the first point in a game, the server begins the next point by serving to the receiver's left-hand court. They continue to shift from right to left with each point until the game is finished. At the end of the first game, the players change ends and they then change ends after each odd-numbered game.

THE DIFFERENCE WITH DOUBLES

The same rules apply for doubles as for singles except that the outer side-lines on the court are used. Thus, the playing area is 33 percent larger. (The area between the singles and doubles sideline is called the alley.)

Each of the four players serves in turn. The pair about to serve in the first game decides which partner will serve first. He serves the first game, the players change ends and one member of the opposing team then serves. The second member of the first pair serves the third game and the second member of the second pair then serves the fourth game. The order of serving is kept throughout the set. The teams change ends after every odd-numbered game.

The receiving team for the first game decides which player will receive the first serve. The other player then receives the second serve, and so on. This order is main-tained throughout the set. In each game, the team members receive serve alternately but, once the ball is in play after the return of serve, either team member can hit the ball.

HOW TO KEEP SCORE

Tennis is scored on three levels—points, games and sets. Generally, the first player to win four points wins the game; the first player to win at least six games, with a margin of at least two games, wins the set; and the first player to win two sets wins the match (except in a few major men's tournaments where a player must win three of five sets).

In a game, both players begin with no score, called love. A player's first point is called 15, the second 30, the third 40 and the fourth wins the game unless both players are even at 40-all, or deuce. After deuce, a player must have a two-point margin to win the game. The first player to score after deuce gains an advantage or ad point. If he loses the next point, the score returns to deuce; if he wins, it's his game. The score is always given with the server's points first; e.g., 40-15 means the server has three points and the receiver one.

If a set is tied at six games all, one more game—called a tiebreaker—can be played to determine the winner rather than continuing until one player goes ahead by two games. Tiebreakers are usually the best of nine or 12 points. It sounds complicated, but don't worry: it all becomes clear when you play.

WHAT YOU NEED TO PLAY

A TENNIS RACQUET

Tennis racquets are made from a variety of materials—wood, metal, fiberglass and graphite are the most popular—but all a beginner needs is a medium-priced wood racquet. It should cost around $35 and will probably be already strung with nylon string by the manufacturer. Seek the advice of a teaching professional or a knowledgeable player before you buy. In the store, have the salesperson check your grip size and test out several models to find one that does not feel heavy in your hand.

TENNIS SHOES

Even as a beginner, you'll have to do a lot of running on the tennis court, so your feet may take quite a pounding. That's why you should buy a top-quality tennis shoe and not discount-store sneakers. A good tennis shoe will have a cushioned insole as well as a lining and padding around the heel and arch to keep your feet comfortable during play.

Shoes with canvas uppers are fine for starting play. Later, you might want to try leather tennis shoes; they're more expensive, but often more durable. Thick socks will cushion your feet and absorb perspiration. Wear your tennis socks when buying tennis shoes to get the best fit. Expect to pay $20 or more for shoes.

TENNIS CLOTHES

You can play tennis in an old T-shirt and cut-off jeans, but you'll feel more comfortable in proper tennis attire. For men, a shirt and a pair of shorts will be enough to get you started. The shirt should be large enough to permit free movement of your arms and the shorts should fit comfortably without chafing. Women can also wear a shirt and shorts, but tennis dresses or separate tops and skirts are more common.

A wide selection of styles and colors is available nowadays, and only a few old-line clubs still insist on the traditional all-white outfit. How much you spend on tennis clothes is a matter of your own personal budget. But there's no need to acquire an extensive wardrobe at first.

TENNIS BALLS

Tennis balls are hollow rubber spheres (usually filled with compressed air or gas to make them bounce) which are covered with a wool and synthetic fiber felt. Balls are generally sold three to a can which is pressurized to keep them factory fresh. Most tennis balls conform to U.S. Tennis Association specifications (look for the words "USTA-Approved" on the can). Depending on their usage, a can of balls lasts a few sets or a few weeks. When the balls begin to lose their bounce, you should open a new can; it's difficult to play tennis with dead balls.

WHERE YOU CAN PLAY

PUBLIC COURTS

More tennis is played on the nation's 100,000 public tennis courts than on any other type of facility. Even small towns often have a couple of courts available in a park or at the local high school.

The quality of public courts ranges from sophisticated, well-maintained operations with locker rooms, instruction and organized tournament play to decrepit facilities with worn-out courts that are unplayable.

The better public courts often support themselves by requiring an inexpensive permit for each player; they'll also offer instruction, may have a court reservation system and may even provide lights for night play. Public courts are the cheapest places to play, but often the most crowded.

INDOOR TENNIS CLUBS

A comparative rarity little more than a decade ago, the indoor tennis clubs have now become almost commonplace in suburban areas in the northern parts of the country. The typical indoor club is a steel-framed structure housing four or more courts, locker rooms, a spectator lounge and a variety of other facilities. Heated in the winter and often air-conditioned in the summer, indoor clubs provide year-round play under consistent conditions.

It all comes at a price; an hour of indoor play can cost anywhere from $15 to more than $50 at peak times. Playing groups frequently rent the same one- or two-hour session each week throughout the winter season. Most indoor clubs offer extensive teaching and clinic programs.

TENNIS AND COUNTRY CLUBS

If you become a keen tennis player and can afford the dues, a private tennis club or country club can be the most agreeable place to play—offering a desirable mix of social and competitive tennis in a pleasant environment.

At a tennis club, of course, the focus is almost exclusively on tennis —although such other sports as swimming and platform tennis may be available, too. At a country club, tennis is usually secondary to golf—although the tennis facilities may be excellent.

Private clubs are expensive:

initiation fees can exceed $1,000 and annual dues can run even higher than that. On the other hand, clubs often provide a range of tennis and other activities for all the family. And the quality of the facilities, the availability of court time and the standard of play will all be better than at public courts.

PRIVATE COURTS

The ultimate facility, of course, is the private court. To build one requires plenty of space (an area of at least 120 feet by 60 feet) and money. It costs $20,000 or so to have a professional court builder put one in; do-it-yourselfers can build one for around $5,000. Playing on a private court can be a delightful social experience and, if you want to be invited back, it always helps to offer

to give your host a hand on clean-up or maintenance after play.

RESORT AND HOTEL COURTS

With the recent boom in the sport, many resorts and hotels have installed tennis facilities to attract guests. However, some hotels may have only a couple of courts, while others have dozens with a full pro shop and an active tennis program for guests. A number of large resorts, moreover, have week-long or weekend clinics that cater to the beginning or low intermediate player.

At many resorts, there's a charge for the use of the courts and, because of the demand, reservations must be made a day or so ahead. Picking the right tennis resort can be tough; for more guidance consult travel directories.

HOW TO GET STARTED

PRIVATE LESSONS

If your pocketbook permits, the best way to learn the sport is through private lessons. Tennis is an individual game that you'll learn fastest by having a qualified teaching professional get you started correctly. He'll show you how to make the best use of your own abilities. Check out your local teaching professionals by asking friends who play and by visiting clubs to observe the pros teach.

As a beginner, you should start with weekly lessons and be sure to practice regularly between them. The number of lessons needed to pick up the game obviously varies from player to player. But even when you can play well, it's a good idea to go back to your pro from time to time for a refresher course and for special instruction on particular shots. Figure on paying $20 or more an hour for a good teaching pro.

GROUP LESSONS

If you have any doubts about your desire to begin playing tennis, then you ought to consider taking a series of group lessons. Most indoor clubs offer them, and many parks and recreation departments have summer tennis classes.

Typically, a teaching pro and one or two assistants will teach a group of 12 or more players. The teaching may be regimented and you may not get much personal attention, but the cost is often low, especially in public parks, and you will meet other players of your own standard with whom you can practice.

TENNIS CAMPS AND CLINICS

Should you prefer a crash course in the game, then a week at a tennis camp or clinic can get you off to a running start. But you'd better be sure that you really do want to learn the sport because they're not cheap and because they can be quite physically demanding.

There are two broad categories of places to go: camps where the accommodations may be fairly spartan and the tennis regimen pretty intense; and clinics where the instruction is no less expert but where the surroundings may be more agreeable since they are usually offered by resorts with a full range of other facilities.

Costs can range from as little as $100 for a two-day weekend tennis camp up to nearly $1,000 for some week-long clinics.

OTHER LEARNING AIDS

When you've had a lesson or two, you'll probably find a tennis instruction book quite useful for reminding you of the ground that you've been covering with your pro. Your local library or bookstore should have a selection of tennis instruction books (or you can order some from the TENNIS Book Service, 495 Westport Ave., Norwalk, CT 06856).

There are also tennis records, tape cassettes and films designed to help you play better.

THE LEVELS OF THE GAME

CLUB PLAY

The essence of tennis is competition and there are tournaments for all types and ages of players from tyros to touring pros.

They begin at the club level. If you join a tennis club, you'll find that it will stage various tournaments throughout the season. There may also be opportunities to play in inter-club matches or in a tennis league. Or you may want to join a tennis ladder where you move up if you beat a player above you and down if you lose to someone below you.

Since there is no absolute standard for measuring tennis ability, it is difficult to determine how you compare to another player without facing him in a match. Until recently, players have been lumped into one of three broad categories: A for advanced players, B for intermediates and C for novices. Early in 1979, however, the National Tennis Rating Program (NTRP) was devised in an attempt to set up a uniform, skill-level determination system for tennis players. Roughly designed to operate like golf's handicap system, the NTRP rates players based on a numerical scale from 1 to 7. It's now used in many areas of the country to help make tournaments and leagues more competitive.

AMATEUR TOURNAMENTS

Beyond the club level, many tournaments are conducted by local parks departments and tennis groups, and for better players by state tennis associations and the U.S. Tennis Association (USTA). There are singles and doubles tournaments for almost everybody—from 12-and-under juniors to 80-and-over seniors, from husband-wife teams to mother-daughter and father-son combinations. One national directory lists more than 2,000 such tournaments every year.

Most of the important amateur events are sanctioned by the USTA and, to play in them, you must be a member of that association. (To apply, write the USTA, 51 East 42nd St., New York, N.Y. 10017.)

PROFESSIONAL CIRCUITS

At the pinnacle of the game are the several hundred men and women professionals who've moved up through the amateur ranks to the international circuit. They roam the world playing in one of the professional tournaments that are held each week. The most prestigious are Wimbledon in England and the U.S. Open in Flushing Meadow, N.Y.

Some particularly gifted amateurs reach the professional level quickly by making it through a few of the qualifying tournaments that precede each major event. Others play on minor tournament circuits, known as satellites, in hopes they'll do well

enough to earn a place in the big-time—much like baseball's minor leaguers.

It's worth the effort. Pro tennis has more than $20 million in prize money up for grabs now each year. The top men players each gross more than $500,000 annually in tournament winnings and receive perhaps two or three times that amount from endorsements, commercials, exhibitions and special events.

The major men's and women's tournaments are each linked by overall point systems; the men's is known as the Volvo Grand Prix and the women's as the Colgate International Series. Players are awarded points according to their performances in each tournament. At the end of the year, the top eight finishers meet in special showdowns. (Operating in conjunction with the Volvo and Colgate Series systems are two other tours: the men's World Championship Tennis circuit, which originally established the men's pro game, and the women's Avon Championships circuit.)

A GUIDE TO WATCHING TENNIS

TOURNAMENT FUNDAMENTALS
Probably the fastest way to develop an appreciation of tennis is to attend a professional or major amateur tournament and observe a number of matches. Or you can learn much from watching tennis on television. It's best to go to a tournament with a knowledgeable tennis friend who can tell you what to look for and help explain things.

Most tennis tournaments are of the single elimination type; that is, when a player loses a match he is eliminated from subsequent rounds of play. The number of players entered in the tournament and their arrangement for the first round of matches is called the draw.

Match pairings for the first round are made by drawing the players' names by lot and placing them on a drawsheet. But the better or seeded players are planted on the drawsheet so that they do not meet each other in early rounds. In major tournaments, the draw is 32—or some multiple of that number of players—so that play progresses in an orderly fashion as the field is halved with each round down to 16 players, then eight (the quarterfinals), four (the semifinals) and two (the final).

Tournaments usually have both singles and doubles competitions, and a major tournament will have a mixed doubles event and possibly events for junior and senior players as well.

MATCH PLAY
When the competitors are evenly matched, the player who is serving has the advantage since he controls the start of the point and can use his serve to put pressure on his opponent. The server, thus, is expected to win his service game.

The receiver, of course, tries to prevent that—to break his opponent's serve. If the receiver goes ahead in a game by the score of 30-40 or better, he is said to have break point; he can break his opponent's serve and win the game by taking the next point.

You will probably be able to sense the tension on court when a break point occurs. That's partly because a player, if he wins his own service games, needs to break his opponent's serve only once to win a set.

When one player is leading with five games, he is said to be playing for the set. If he gets to within one point of winning the next game, he has set point. The pressure is often such that a player will make an error and lose that chance to win the set. He may make a series of errors, permitting his opponent to come back and win the set. It is this ebb and flow of the game that makes tennis a fascinating spectator sport.

An even more tense situation occurs when a player gets within a few points of winning two sets and, hence, the match. When a player is only one point away from victory, he has match point. These points can be the hardest to play, even for seasoned professionals. And you'll feel these tensions yourself when you begin to play competitively—even if it's only with your neighbor.

THE OFFICIALS
In a major tournament match, there are many more officials than players. Controlling the match is an umpire who sits in an elevated chair at one end of the net, records and announces scores, arbitrates disputes and sees to it that play proceeds within the rules.

He is assisted by linesmen whose job it is to determine whether a ball lands inside or outside of the lines they are assigned to watch. Calling the lines is a demanding task that calls for keen eyesight and concentration.

Players sometimes question line calls and even ask for the removal of a linesman whom they believe is performing inadequately. Such disputes are resolved by the referee, a tournament official who decides on matters of tournament policy and rarely becomes involved in the actual play.

POINTS TO WATCH
After you've grasped the basics of tournament play, you'll learn more that will help you as a tennis player if you concentrate on watching just one player at a time and not just the flight of the ball back and forth over the net. The best place to sit at a tennis match is in the bleachers (if there are any) behind either of the baselines.

Sit above the players; the vantage point that the TV cameras use for overall court shots is about right. Now you can focus on one player and not lose sight of his opponent. In fact, you can put yourself in the position of the player you are watching. How would you have played that last point?

Watch the server carefully. You'll note that the placement of the serve will vary. Often, if the receiver has a weak shot, many of the serves will go to that weaker side. Note, too, that a player's second serve will often seem to curve into the court; that's because the player has made the ball spin to make sure it goes into the service box and yet gives his opponent a difficult ball to return.

In men's tennis in particular, you'll notice that the server will often follow his ball toward the net so that he can hit the receiver's return before it bounces; that is, volley the ball. This serve-and-volley style of tennis puts great pressure on a receiver to hit a good return of serve, but requires skill, speed and experience to do consistently well.

You'll see other players who prefer what's known as the backcourt or baseline game. The player will remain at his own baseline after he serves and attempt to outduel his opponent.

Nonetheless, even the better baseline players will go to the net when the opportunity arises because it's the quickest way to polish off a point. They'll move up when an opponent sends them a short ball (one that lands around the service line), hit an approach shot deep into the other court and then proceed to a volleying position at the net.

Make it a point, too, to watch player movement on the court. Sure, the pros have superb strokes, but it doesn't do them any good if they can't get to the ball to use their strokes. So notice that they're never still between shots in a rally. They're always moving, always trying to anticipate where the next shot will come. That's why they generally manage to be in the right place at the right time.

Try to learn a little as you enjoy a tournament match. It will assist your own development as a player.

TENNIS CONCEPTS EVERY PLAYER SHOULD KNOW

On the face of it, tennis seems to be a rather simple sport—merely a matter of hitting a ball back and forth over a net into a reasonably large area. But as any tennis player can attest, there's quite a bit more to it than that.

It takes hours of practice to reach a point where you can stroke a ball smoothly and consistently. But beyond that, the complexities of the game require that you understand what happens to the ball as it flies through the air and how your movements and those of the other players influence the course of play.

This chapter explains the fundamental concepts of tennis that you should appreciate before you begin playing—or perhaps review even if you already know the game. An understanding of the principles will help you learn the game more quickly and thoroughly.

On the next two pages, we examine the three primary ways to hit a tennis ball (with each demonstrated by Ron Holmberg). Then, on succeeding pages, there's an explanation of the flight of the ball and, finally, an elementary look at the ways players move around the court.

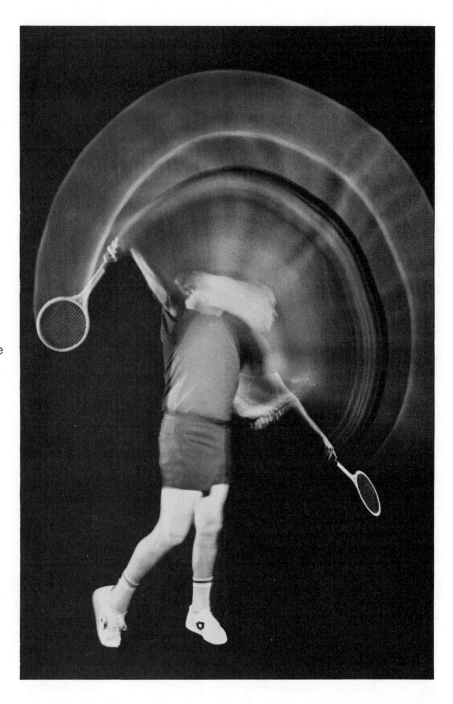

HOW THE RACQUET MOVES: THE 3 BASIC SWINGS

THE OVERHEAD STROKES

Two tennis strokes are hit with an overhead motion—the serve and the smash. The action for both is very similar: the player takes his racquet back behind his head (the backswing) and then brings it up in an almost circular motion (the forward swing) to hit the ball when the racquet is almost as high as the player can reach. The swing continues across the player's body (the follow-through) until the head of the racquet is pointing behind him. The follow-through for a serve is shown from the side and above in the photos at right.

The major difference in the two strokes is that to serve, the player places the ball in the air with a lifting motion (not shown in the photos).

Although it requires some coordination to get the ball and the racquet in the right place at the right time, the serve is easier than the smash because the player can take his time with the shot.

By contrast, the smash is hit off a ball that the opposing player has lofted high in the air—using a lob (see ground strokes, below)—usually to force a player away from the net and to give the hitter time to recover his position. Since the lobbed ball is likely to drop rapidly, a player attempting a smash must carefully judge the flight of the ball and time the stroke to hit it properly. Thus, the smash is often considered to be a relatively advanced stroke; in fact, an effective smash is one of the hallmarks of a good player.

However, both the serve and the smash are powerful strokes and derive much of their power from the long swing. When a player takes the racquet well back, he can snap his wrist forward to accelerate the racquet head into the swing so that it will move faster than on the other tennis strokes. Some professional players can serve the ball so hard that it leaves the racquet at more than 125 miles per hour.

It's also important for the player to keep the racquet moving immediately after hitting the ball, even though the racquet is no longer in contact with the ball. Otherwise, the racquet head would be slowing down during the hit. So an effective serve or overhead must be hit with a long and continuous follow-through.

THE GROUND STROKES

The ground strokes (so-called because the ball bounces on the ground before the player hits it) are also long strokes, but executed with a semi-circular motion made on a nearly horizontal plane for the most part (see photos on the right). The two major ground strokes—and the backbones of most tennis players' games—are the forehand (shown in the two photos on the right) and the backhand (a shot like the forehand but hit on the opposite side of the body).

To hit a ground stroke, the player takes his racquet back behind him (the backswing) and then brings it forward to hit the ball (the forward swing). He then allows the racquet

to continue so that the head finishes out in front of his body (the follow-through).

Like the overhead strokes, the ground strokes must be full; the player must get his racquet back early so that he has enough time to swing it forward and hit the ball about halfway through the stroke—usually just a little in front of his body. The power of a ground stroke comes largely from the long forward swing, a forward weight transfer and a full follow-through. As with the overhead strokes, the long follow-through helps ensure that the racquet head does not slow down before or during contact with the ball.

The swing on the ground strokes should be smooth and continuous.

The pros with the classical strokes, such as Vitas Gerulaitis on the forehand or Evonne Goolagong on the backhand, have a fluid motion that almost makes the racquet flow into the ball and is quite beautiful to watch. Such players "hit through the ball;" that is, they try to maintain contact with the ball for as long as possible so that they can control its direction and yet hit a powerful shot.

Both the forehand and the backhand are usually hit with a slight upward motion to make sure that the ball clears the net by a respectable margin. When a player wants to hit a lob (a very high ball), he exaggerates the lifting motion at contact and into the follow-through. The swing, though, is still largely semi-circular.

THE VOLLEYS

The forehand and backhand volleys are the shortest strokes in tennis. They are used to hit the ball in flight before it bounces in the court. Most volleys are hit from quite close to the net where there is little time to get into position and use the long swing that's employed for the ground strokes. That's not required, however, because there's less need for power since a volleyed ball will often have a shorter distance to travel.

The arc of a volley swing is no more than a quarter of a circle, as the photos of a forehand volley show

on the right. The backswing is very compact and the racquet is brought forward quickly to hit the ball in front of the body. On the backhand volley, the ball may be hit even farther in front because the arm does not have to cross in front of the player's body.

On most volleys, the racquet head moves on a slight downward plane (see photo opposite) since the player is often hitting down on a rising ball. That downward motion will produce a little underspin (or backward rotation) on the ball which helps control the shot and will produce a low bounce in the opponent's court. The stroke is

similar for a low volley—one taken below net level. But the racquet face is tilted backward more to enable the ball to rise so it can clear the net.

The essence of the volley is that it is a compact stroke with a forward punching action designed to place the ball quickly and, frequently, to win the point. Many beginning players feel that volleys are harder to master than the ground strokes. It's true that volleying does require a certain knack in timing that comes with practice. Once that's achieved, volleying is often easier than hitting a ground stroke.

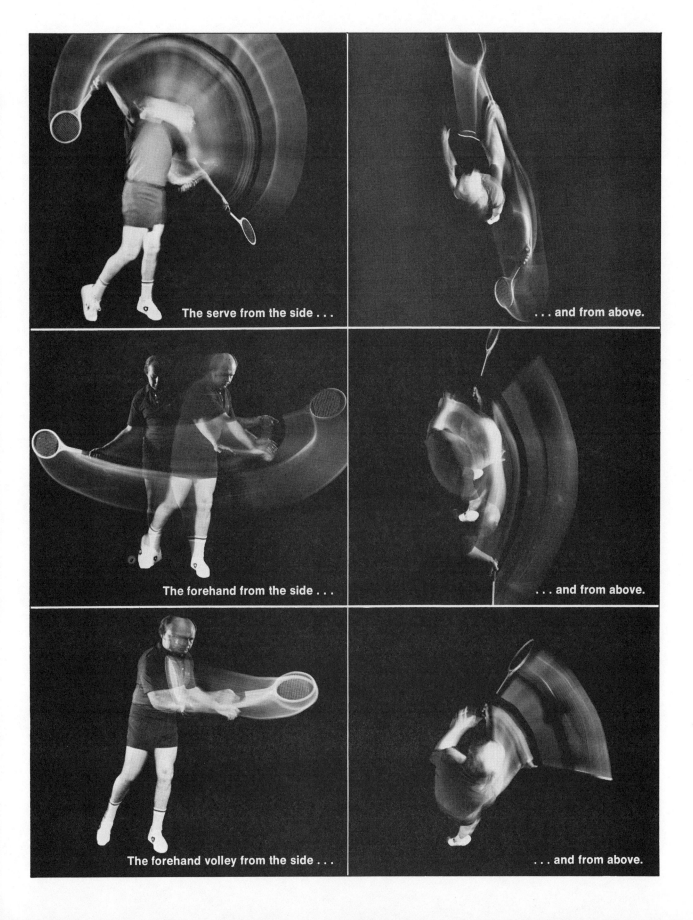

The serve from the side . . .

. . . and from above.

The forehand from the side . . .

. . . and from above.

The forehand volley from the side . . .

. . . and from above.

HOW THE BALL MOVES: THE PRINCIPLES OF FLIGHT

THE SERVE AND OVERHEAD

The flight of the ball is similar for both the serve and the overhead. The ball is contacted high in the air, travels almost horizontally at first, and then descends into the opponent's court as air resistance slows the ball down and the pull of gravity takes over.

The serve is always hit from the baseline and must land within the diagonally opposite service court; so the ball may travel as much as 60 feet before bouncing. The flight of an overhead smash can also be quite long if hit from the backcourt to go deep into the opposing court.

Many beginners have a hard time getting their serves over the net, and many an overhead smash is pounded into the net. The reason is that the hitter did not realize that the ball must be hit forward, and not down, in order to carry the necessary distance over the net. On a serve or a deep smash, the first part of the ball's flight should be almost horizontal to make sure that the ball goes over the net. As the ball slows down, it will drop faster and curve into the court or the service box.

THE GROUND STROKES

The objective with a ground stroke is usually to send the ball almost the length of the court (78 feet)—whether the ball is hit as a forehand or backhand drive or as a lob.

Many beginners delight in hitting screaming drives that just skim over the net. It's a satisfying feeling when the shots land in bounds, but it's also an invitation to disaster. The chances of the ball clearing the net are reduced, and should one catch the top of the net and skip over, it will generally land short in the other court.

To send the ball deep, it's necessary to hit it so that it passes several feet above the net. As with the serve, air resistance will slow the ball and gravity will then pull it down into the court. So as a rule, the higher the ball is hit over the net, the deeper it will go into the opposing court. If it's hit too high, of course, it may go out.

A deep lob also has to travel the length of the court but be high enough to give you time enough to get back into position. Many beginners make the mistake of hitting a lob with too much upward motion. A lob must be hit upward and forward to go the length of the court.

THE VOLLEYS

Volleys have the simplest trajectory of all tennis shots. Generally, the ball has only a short distance to travel and, ideally, it is hit from above the level of the net down into the opposing court.

A short, angled volley must be placed accurately and not overhit so that it goes out of court. Some better players put a little underspin on the shot so that the ball will stay low and be tougher for the opponent to reach.

Deeper volleys may have to travel half the length of the court. So the ball should be hit forward and out to make it go deep. As with the ground strokes, gravity will pull the ball down as it slows through the air.

Low volleys are considerably more difficult to execute because the player has to hit the ball up over the net from a position relatively close to it. If there's too little upward motion, the ball will go into the net. If there's too much upward motion, the ball will fly up into the air—and either sail past the baseline or provide an easy target for the opponent.

SERVE

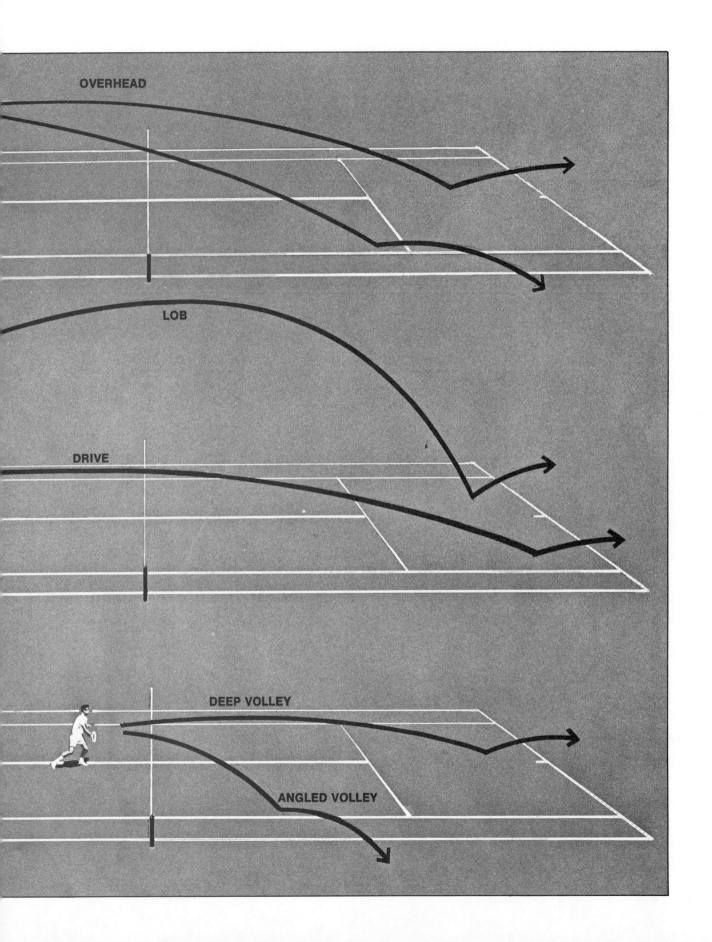

HOW THE PLAYERS MOVE: THE IMPORTANCE OF POSITION

WHEN SERVING

The serve is the one time in tennis when a player has complete control of his destiny. As a server, he can take time to prepare fully, to decide how and where to hit the ball, and to work out where to position himself after serving.

So, before delivering the ball, the server should decide whether he would prefer to play out the point from the baseline or at the net. Playing at the baseline is usually a defensive game while playing at the net is usually an offensive game.

If the server (shown in the foreground above) decides to stay back, he should move to a position about three feet behind the baseline, roughly midway between the sidelines (A).

From there, he will be able to move quickly to either side, if necessary, to return his opponent's shots.

If the server decides to go to the net, he should dart forward immediately after he serves the ball so that he is close to the "T" formed by the service line and the center service line (B) when the receiver is about to hit the ball. Usually the server will slow momentarily at that point, see where the return of serve is going and then move to cut off the ball before it bounces with a volley. This style of play is called serve and volley and is the mark of a better player, especially in singles, since it calls

for both sound strokes and deft footwork.

By contrast, the receiver (in the far court in this drawing) will usually stay back behind the baseline after returning serve (C). Generally, the receiver will try to hit deep balls in the hope of forcing the server into making an error and losing the point. However, an aggressive player will often look for a short ball (one that bounces closer to the service line than the baseline) so that he can advance to a volleying position close to the net (D) after hitting his approach shot.

When the server comes in, the receiver will often hit a shorter ball directly to the server's feet. That kind of a ball is hard to return for an oncoming server.

AT THE BASELINE

Playing from the baseline usually calls for a conservative style of play based on simply getting the ball back over the net and deep into the opponent's court. Even at the professional level, few winning, unreturnable shots are hit from the baseline. Points are won or lost on errors when a player hits a ball out of court or into the net. Consequently, a baseline player should have a reliable and consistent game.

After serving, a baseline player will normally return to a position behind the baseline and close to the center mark (A) so that he can move quickly to return balls hit on either side of him. A good opponent will often hit balls alternately to each corner (B and C) to force the baseliner to run to make a return. Shots hit on the run are often weak ones—so the chance for error is increased.

When playing against a baseliner with good ground strokes, an opponent will often hit shorter balls to force the other player to come to the net (D) where he may feel less confident and, as a result, be more likely to make an error.

The baseliner can be in trouble if he's pulled into the area between the baseline and the service line (E). That's known as "no-man's land" because it's a dangerous area where the player may have to handle tough balls that land at his feet. It's vital to flee it as quickly as possible—either by moving on up to the net to hit a volley on the next shot or by retreating back behind the baseline, which can be difficult.

AT THE NET

Net play is probably the most difficult style of tennis to master. But once that's done, it increases a player's chances of winning quite significantly.

Close to the net, most balls have to be volleyed, that is, hit before they bounce, which calls for quick reactions and accurate stroke-making. One or two volleys should win most points, though, since the player at the net is in a position to hit the ball so quickly at—or out of the reach of —his opponent. That's why better players constantly try to control the game from close to the net, particularly on faster courts where the ball doesn't bounce very high.

A net player should position him-self close to the center of the court about halfway between the service line and the net (A). Generally, the more aggressive the player, the closer he will get to the net. His objective is to hit a volley that his opponent cannot return (as the player in the near court is doing here).

His opponent can attempt to beat the net player in several ways. One of the most common is with a passing shot—a hard forehand or backhand drive that travels out of reach to one side or other of the net player (B). That means the net player must be ready to move, usually on a diagonal path (C and D) to cut off any antici-pated passing shots.

Or the opponent at the baseline may hit a lob over the net player's head (E), forcing him to retreat toward the baseline in order to return it (F). The net player can do that with an overhead smash. But if the lob is so high and deep that he can't reach it, he'll have to scramble back and try to retrieve the ball on the bounce —thus, surrendering his position at the net. So the net player can't afford to get too close to the net or a lob is likely to elude him completely.

STROKING/PLATEAU ONE

HOW TO HIT A FOREHAND

A BASIC STROKE

Every player's game is built upon three basic strokes: the forehand drive, the backhand drive and the serve. They are where tennis begins for all players because, with some mastery of them, it is possible to start to play the game and experience the rewards of competition.

The forehand is usually the first stroke attempted by beginners because it seems the most "natural." All the action takes place unimpeded right in front of the body and the

motion of the swing is a familiar one. It's one all of us have used many times—in swiping at a pile of blocks as toddlers, for example, or in beating a rug or in hitting a baseball or a softball. Indeed, anyone with a background in games involving a bat and ball can acquire a respectable forehand very quickly.

So for many players, the forehand becomes their strongest, most consistent stroke—the one that can be relied on most of the time. But

because the stroke comes relatively easily to many players, it is all too easy for them to develop bad habits, ones that can be damaging as they move up the competitive ladder. That's why it's vital to learn the forehand correctly at the start and not depend solely on natural instinct to provide the proper form. It's vital, too, for experienced players to check their forehands—and other strokes as well—from time to time to make sure that they are still following the correct basics.

SHAKE HANDS
WITH THE RACQUET

Proper stroking starts with a proper grip. If you learn to hold the racquet correctly, it will feel comfortable in your hand and you will be able to hit the ball where you want it to go with some oomph on it. An incorrect grip not only produces poorer shots; it can also be difficult to alter later.

The best way to hold the racquet to hit a forehand is the Eastern forehand, or "shake-hands" grip, so-

called because you clasp the handle as if you were shaking hands with your racquet. In fact, one way to get the proper forehand grip is to have someone hand you a racquet, butt end first, with the racquet face vertical. Simply grip the racquet's handle as though you were shaking hands.

A better, and more reliable way is to hold your racquet by its throat with your other hand and put the palm of your gripping hand flat on the racquet strings (see photo, above). Then, slide your hand down the shaft until you can close your hand around the handle with the fleshy part of the base of your palm up against the butt of the handle. Spread your index finger ahead of the thumb to hold the racquet firmly.

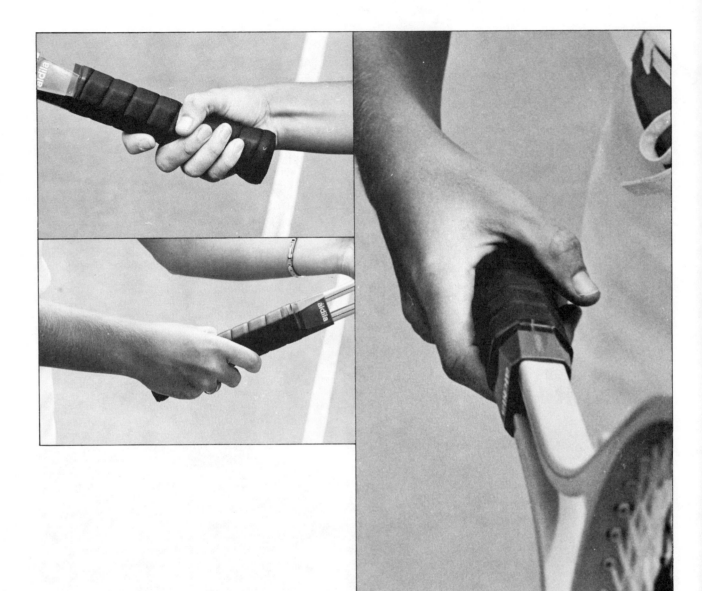

CHECK YOUR GRIP

If you are holding the racquet in the proper Eastern grip, your fingers should be spread apart slightly so that the racquet is a normal extension of your arm (see photos above).

Be sure, too, that the "V" formed by your thumb and index finger is directly over the edge where the top of the racquet handle meets the right bevel (see photo above) or the left bevel if you're left-handed. You can make this quick check as you adopt the ready position, waiting for your opponent to hit the ball.

ASSUME THE
READY POSITION

When you are behind the baseline waiting for your opponent to hit the ball, you should get in a position that will prepare you to move quickly in any direction to hit the ball. The ready position, as it's called, is a little like a boxer's crouch.

To get in the ready position (demonstrated below by Stan Smith), take a relaxed stance with your feet about shoulder width apart, your knees bent and your upper body leaning forward slightly. If you lean forward a little, you'll put your weight onto the balls of your feet.

Keep your racquet up and pointed ahead of you so that it can be moved to either side quickly to prepare for your stroke. The racquet head should be a little above waist level.

KEYS TO THE FOREHAND

TURN YOUR SHOULDERS

Many beginners make the mistake of waiting too long before they move their racquets to prepare to hit the ball. Decide whether you are going to hit a forehand (or a backhand) before the ball crosses the net on its way to you. Then, as soon as you make that decision, turn your shoulders and upper body so that you begin to get yourself sideways to the net.

As you turn your upper body (see photo at right), your racquet arm will also turn; thus, you will start taking the racquet back almost automatically. That means if the ball comes to you faster than expected, you can still get the racquet back quickly and make a respectable shot.

When you turn your shoulders, remember to keep looking at the oncoming ball. Never turn your head around so that you lose sight of the ball. You must watch the ball throughout the stroke.

GET YOUR RACQUET BACK EARLY

Preparation is the key to success with your strokes, and the problems many beginners have can be traced to poor or late preparation. There's one simple cure: get your racquet back as soon as you can and take it all the way back until it's pointing at the back fence (see photo at right). If you prepare early, you'll always have lots of time to hit the ball.

How you get the racquet back is not as important as getting it back early and starting the forward swing from a position just below the flight of the ball. Some players favor a straight backswing, others a gentle loop. It's largely a matter of personal preference, but most beginners will find a straight backswing easier.

When you practice your forehands, have someone check that you are taking your racquet all the way back and that you are keeping the racquet head just below waist level at the end of the backswing.

HIT THROUGH THE BALL

For a powerful forehand, you must "hit through the ball," which is a tennis player's way of saying keep the racquet strings and the ball in contact for as long as possible. Hitting through the ball not only helps put power into the shot; but on top of that, the longer the ball and your racquet strings are in contact, the more control you will have over the shot.

To hit the ball, bring your racquet forward on a slightly rising path that starts from a little below your waist and comes up to waist height at about the point of contact with the ball. As you swing forward, shift your weight from your back foot to your front foot. Proper weight transfer is an important element of the stroke; it will add power to your shot.

Now, meet the ball just opposite your front knee (see photo at right), using a smooth stroke that continues out in front of you in the direction that you'd like the ball to go.

FINISH YOUR
FOLLOW-THROUGH

Keep your racquet moving forward after the ball leaves the strings. Make the racquet follow the ball's flight for as long as you can and, then, let your arm and the racquet come naturally around your body until the racquet head finishes high in front of you (see photo at right).

If you know you're going into a long follow-through, you won't slow the racquet head down as you meet the ball. As a result, you'll be assured of hitting through it for as long as possible. A complete follow-through will also turn your body to face the net so that you can track the departing ball and get back into the ready position again to prepare for your opponent's next shot.

When you finish your follow-through, your weight should be completely on your front foot. But you should still be well balanced and ready to make your next move.

THE FOREHAND AT A GLANCE

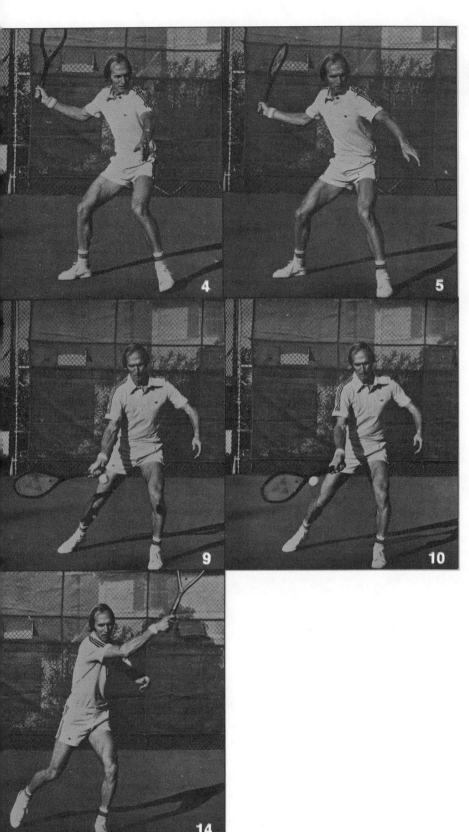

How it's done: Stan Smith demon-strates the full, flowing swing of a powerful forehand in this high-speed photo sequence.

FOREHAND FOOTWORK

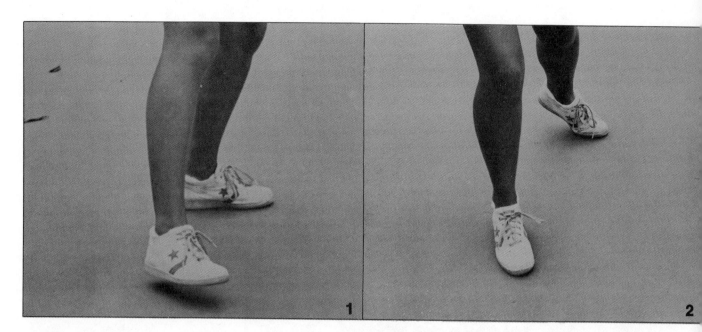

USE SHORT STEPS

When you first start to learn the forehand drive, your teacher will probably toss balls to you so that all you have to do is step toward the ball and make your hit. But in actual play, few shots will be that easy. Usually, you will have to move several steps to get into position to hit the ball. Many beginners find it difficult both to move to the ball and then to hit it.

The key is to get into position smartly, taking your racquet back as you move. From the ready position (shown from the side in photo 1 above), move rapidly sideways using short steps (2) until you get close to the expected line of flight of the oncoming ball. Unless the ball goes wide to one of the corners of the court, it's rarely necessary to turn and run hard for the ball. Short, skipping steps are all that you'll need.

When you get close to the point where you can intercept the ball, plant your right foot (left if you're a left-hander) firmly and begin to step toward the net as you start your forward swing (3). This last step should bring you close to the ball at the moment of contact and bring your weight forward into the shot as you hit the ball.

As you follow through after contact, you should have all your weight on your front foot (4). Use the toes of your back foot to help maintain your balance. And don't take too big a final step toward the ball or you may very well wind up off-balance and, thus, lose valuable time in getting ready for your next shot.

Watch the departing ball, but don't spend time admiring your shot. If you've had to move away from a central baseline position, scramble quickly back to that spot using those same short, skipping steps and regain your ready position.

Remember that tennis is a game of movement. You can't hit the ball if you can't get to it. So work on your footwork as well as your strokes.

Forehand/Checklist
1. Keep your eyes on the ball.
2. Use the Eastern forehand ("shake hands") grip.
3. Get your racquet back early and draw it all the way back.
4. Hit firmly and smoothly through the ball, keeping it on your racquet strings for as long as possible.
5. Finish your stroke with a long follow-through across your body.
6. Resume your central ready position as soon as you've finished your stroke.

HOW TO HIT A BACKHAND

A NATURAL STROKE
Too many tennis beginners—and more experienced players, too, for that matter—are intimidated by the backhand. It seems awkward, some-how, to hit the ball on the "other" side of the body; the forehand seems more comfortable partly because it resembles the familiar swing that's used in hitting a baseball.

But the backhand stroke shouldn't be all that unfamiliar. The motion resembles the one used for ring-tossing or throwing a Frisbee. In fact, the long follow-through of a Frisbee toss is almost exactly the action required for a good backhand ground stroke. So it's unlikely that the back-hand will be completely novel to a new tennis player.

It's vital for the novice to resist temptation and to bear down on practicing the backhand as much as

the forehand. Otherwise, he'll build a weakness into his game right from the start. Besides, most better players will tell you that the backhand is their more reliable ground stroke. That's because the motion involves a natural opening of the body as the racquet swings through the stroke. By contrast, the forehand has a cramping action as the arm comes across the body.

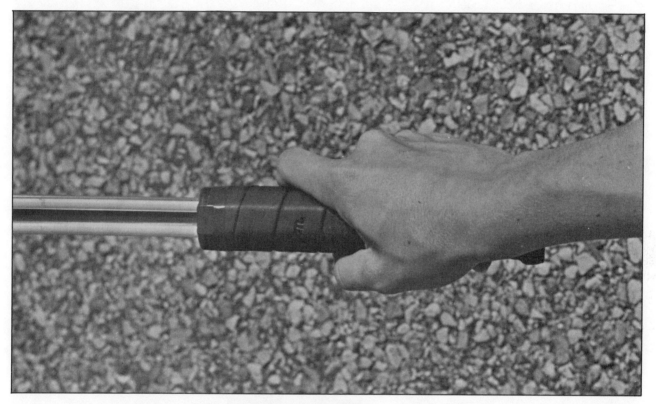

CHANGE YOUR GRIP

If you use a proper Eastern forehand "shake hands" grip to hit a forehand, you'll have to change your grip for a backhand. Using a forehand grip would tilt the racquet face back too much and cause you to hit the ball up in the air.

So you should rotate your hand about a quarter turn over the top of the racquet for the Eastern backhand grip. That will put the meaty part of your thumb behind the racquet handle so that you can swing the racquet toward the ball with the face tilted only slightly back as you hit (see above).

KEYS TO THE BACKHAND

ROTATE YOUR UPPER BODY
The ready position is exactly the same for both the forehand and backhand. You should wait with your weight slightly forward and your racquet held out in front. You should be ready to move quickly to either side. Most players wait with a forehand grip. Then, once they see the ball is coming to the backhand side, they quickly rotate the racquet to a backhand grip.

When you decide that you are going to hit a backhand, turn your shoulders and upper body so that you start to get yourself sideways to the net (see photo at right). Turning your upper body first will start your racquet moving back and will get you better prepared to hit the ball early.

As you turn your shoulders, keep your eyes firmly fixed on the oncoming ball. Don't let your head turn so that you momentarily lose sight of the ball. Watch the ball throughout the stroke.

GET YOUR RACQUET ALL THE WAY BACK

You should use a long, smooth forward swing on the backhand—as you do on the forehand—for a powerful, controlled shot. So you should take your racquet well back when you prepare for a backhand. And, of course, you should take your racquet back as early as you can.

Some players prefer to take the racquet straight back, using the other hand as a guide to make sure that the head stays a bit below the point where you intend to contact the oncoming ball. Other players favor a slightly elliptical swing. A looping swing will often produce more top-spin, but a beginner will probably find the straight backswing is simpler and easier.

You should also keep your elbow comfortably close to your body on the backswing (as Billie Jean King shows her student in the photo at right). That will help prevent you from hitting with a flicking action.

MEET THE BALL OUT IN FRONT

You should bring your racquet forward on a slightly rising plane to make contact with the ball. That way, you'll put a little natural topspin on your shot which will help you control the ball's direction and bring it down safely into your opponent's court.

The backhand motion produces a natural opening action of the body. And that makes it easy to hit the ball out in front of your forward foot (see photo at right) where you should. You can not only see the ball better out there; you also have more flexibility in placing it because you're meeting it ahead—instead of beside or behind your body.

Meet the ball with a firm wrist by gripping the racquet handle a little more tightly as you hit through the ball. A loose wrist can result in a weak or erratic shot, while a firm wrist will give you a powerful shot when you hit the ball solidly in the middle of the strings.

USE A HIGH
FOLLOW-THROUGH

Your body should uncoil like a spring
as you hit the ball and move into the
follow-through. It's rather like the way
a baseball batter brings both his
shoulders and the bat around
together to get the most power into
his swing.

Keep your racquet moving after
you hit the ball until you finish the
follow-through with your racquet high
in front of you (see photo at right). If
you abbreviate the follow-through,
the chances are that the racquet
head will be slowing down as you hit
the ball—which will result in a less
powerful shot.

You should finish your stroke with
your feet still sideways to the net but
with your upper body facing forward.
Your weight will be on your front foot
but you should be balanced and
ready to move quickly back into a
central position behind the baseline
so you can reply to your opponent's
next shot.

THE BACKHAND AT A GLANCE

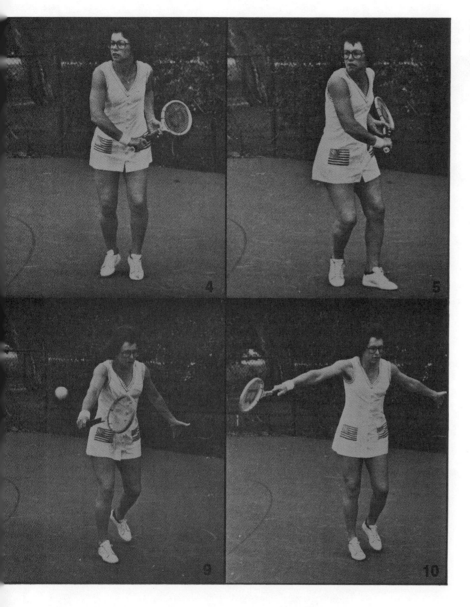

How it's done: Billie Jean King shows the proper form for a reliable backhand in this high-speed photo sequence.

BACKHAND FOOTWORK

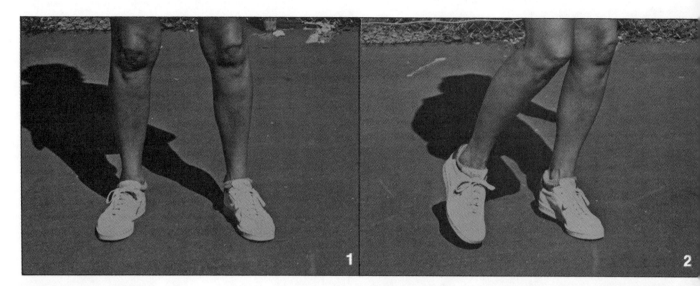

1

2

MOVING ON COURT

Good footwork is the foundation of good forehands and backhands—just as it is, of course, of all strokes. While it is relatively easy to turn and hit a ball that comes more or less directly to you, many players have problems when they have to move to a wider ball. So it's important that you use the correct footwork from the start.

From the ready position (photo 1 above), you should move sideways with short, skipping steps (2) until you get close to the expected line of flight of the ball. When the ball is hit very wide, you may have to turn and run with longer steps and then take short, quick steps to adjust your hitting position.

When you're close to the point where you're going to hit the ball, plant your back foot firmly (3) and start to step toward the net as you begin your forward swing. This step will help you get your weight moving forward into the shot to put extra power into it. You'll be pushing off your back foot while still keeping it in contact with the ground for balance.

When you finish your stroke (4), all your weight should be on your front foot. However, you should be balanced and ready to recover for your next shot. Make sure that your back foot stays in contact with the court throughout your follow-through. If you lose your balance, you may take so long to recover that your opponent will be able to put the ball away.

So as soon as you've completed your follow-through, move quickly back into a ready position just behind the baseline approximately midway between the sidelines. If you've had to move away from the central position, scramble back with the same short skipping steps you used to chase the ball and resume your ready stance. Keep your eyes on the ball as you move back into position and be ready to move when your opponent hits the ball.

Remember that tennis is a game of movement. You can't hit the ball if you can't get to it. So work on your footwork as well as your strokes.

Backhand/Checklist
1. Watch the ball throughout the stroke.
2. Rotate your racquet for a full backhand grip.
3. Turn your shoulders to start your racquet back early.
4. Hit through the ball with a firm wrist.
5. Complete your stroke with a full follow-through high and in front of your body.
6. Recover to a central ready position just behind the baseline.

HOW TO HIT A BASIC SERVE

THE CRITICAL STROKE
The serve is generally considered the most important shot in tennis. It's used to start every point and can effectively determine what happens after that. So it's vital for every player to develop an accurate, consistent delivery—one that enables him to capitalize on the advantage he enjoys when serving.

The shot, to be sure, requires good timing and body coordination. But it's easier because you can control the ball's position until you put it into play.

There are fewer variables to contend with because you are not returning a shot hit by your opponent. When you're serving, you start the action. You have time to set up properly and there's no reason for you to have to hurry your service motion.

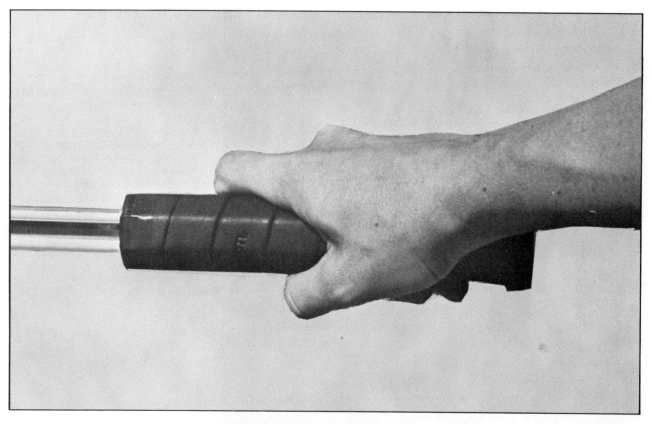

USE A MID-WAY GRIP

Although many advanced players use a backhand grip on the serve, beginners will find it easier to use a grip halfway between the Eastern forehand (or "shake hands") grip and the Eastern backhand grip. With this grip, you'll be able to put some natural spin on the ball, which will help bring it down into the service box after it has safely cleared the net.

To arrive at the proper grip, first grasp the racquet handle as if you were shaking hands with it. (That's the Eastern forehand grip.) Then, rotate your hand over the top of the racquet until the "V" formed by your thumb and forefinger is centered on the top panel of the handle (see photo above).

STARTING THE SERVICE MOTION

TAKE THE PROPER STANCE

When serving, it's important that you first assume a relaxed, comfortable position behind the baseline, near the center mark. Your weight should be placed on your front foot, and both your hands and the racquet should be held at about chest level.

Stand with your feet about shoulder-width apart and your front foot placed at about 45 degrees to the baseline. If you've set your feet properly, you should be sideways to the net so that a line drawn from toe to toe would point directly to the court where you're about to serve.

Your feet should be positioned this way whether you are standing close to the center mark where you should be when serving in singles, or between the center mark and the singles sideline, where you should be for the serve in doubles. Keep your front foot about three inches behind the baseline so you don't foot fault.

PLACE THE BALL
IN FRONT OF YOU

The service motion requires the coordination of two different arm movements: placing the ball into the air with one arm and, then, bringing your racquet up to make contact with the other arm. Ideally, your racquet arm should be fully outstretched when you hit the ball. And to do that, you have to release the ball properly.

Before you begin practicing the ball release, you should consider where you want to place the ball.

Your objective is to position the ball so that if you were to let it drop to the ground without hitting it, the ball would land about one to two feet inside the baseline and to the right of your front foot (or left if you're left-handed).

In other words, don't release the ball directly overhead. If you do, the chances are that the ball will be behind you when you make contact with it. Remember, you want to hit the ball out in front, so place it out in front.

RELEASE THE BALL GENTLY

Once you've determined where you want the ball to go after it leaves your hand, the next step is to practice your ball release until it becomes nearly automatic.

The key is to release the ball in such a way that it peaks at, or just a bit higher than, the projected contact point. That way, you can hit the ball when it's practically motionless.

Now, hold the ball lightly on the tips of your thumb and your first three fingers with your racquet held alongside in your hand at about chest level. Then, drop both arms together toward your front knee. From that position, move your ball arm up in a straight path out in front of you toward the right net post (for right-handers), lifting the ball in as vertical a line as possible.

When your arm reaches about eye level, the ball should leave your hand with an almost imperceptible opening of the fingertips that imparts no spin to the rising ball (see photo at right).

AN OPTIONAL SERVE
FOR BEGINNERS

If you've never served before, or are a beginner who has experienced some timing and coordination difficulties hitting conventional serves, you can try a simpler stroke, using an abbreviated service motion.

The key to this simplified motion is to get your racquet head down behind your back as far as you comfortably can, before you start the ball release.

Next, release the ball and, as it nears its peak, start your racquet up and over your shoulder. Make contact in front of your body. During the forward swing, transfer your weight to your front foot and snap your wrist forward at impact. That will help you put as much zing on the serve as you can.

But it will still lack the authority of a conventional serve. That's why it's only recommended for beginners or those who have trouble coordinating the arm movements required for a normal serving motion.

THE BALL TOSS AT A GLANCE

The ball release: Vic Seixas demonstrates the smooth arm movement and delicate touch needed to position the ball accurately.

MEETING THE BALL SQUARELY

DRAW THE RACQUET BACK
The complete, conventional service motion differs from the abbreviated serve in that it requires greater arm coordination. As one arm is being raised to release the ball, the other should be taking the racquet back and up.

From the ready stance (see photo at right), you begin moving your ball arm upward to release the ball while your other arm takes the racquet up and back in as big an arc, or loop, as possible. Get the elbow of your racquet arm up, away from your body (as demonstrated in the photo below), because that will help you get the proper arc on your swing and, therefore, more leverage on the swing.

During your backswing, shift your weight to your back foot. This kind of rocking motion can be helpful in establishing a natural rhythm for the stroke. If you find this motion difficult, start the serve with your weight on your back foot.

SCRATCH YOUR BACK

To put some power into the serve, you should take your racquet up and back as far as possible on the backswing. When you near the top of the backswing, flex your arm and wrist to bring the racquet head down behind your back.

Lifting your elbow on the backswing will help you take your racquet back far enough and get your wrist properly cocked. Try to get the head of the racquet down as far as you can, into what is commonly referred to as the "backscratching position." It's not easy for all players to get their racquets in that position and, indeed, it's not absolutely necessary. But the farther you bring your racquet down behind you, the harder you're able to hit the ball.

When the racquet is back and your elbow is at about shoulder level, you'll be ready to bring it forward with a throwing-type motion that will help you put power into your serve.

REACH TO MAKE
SOLID CONTACT

With your arm in the backscratching position, your body should be coiled like a spring and your shoulders should point toward the service box where you want the ball to go. Start the forward swing by bringing the racquet upward over your shoulder, keeping your wrist cocked. Your body should be slightly arched and your knees bent a little at this point.

Try to time your swing so that you make contact with the ball in front of your body. At impact, snap your wrist forward from its cocked position. Your arm should be fully extended. As you hit the ball, your body should be leaning well into the court and be stretched out in almost a straight line from your fingers to your ankles, so that if you were to drop the racquet, it would land well inside the baseline (see photo at right).

MOVE YOUR
WEIGHT FORWARD

Proper weight transfer during the service motion plays an important role in determining the power and accuracy of your serves. Without it, the best you can expect are weak serves that are hit only with the arm motion and wrist snap.

When your racquet is coming up from behind your back, your weight should begin moving off your back foot and onto your front foot. This weight transfer enhances the uncoiling action of your body as your knees and arched back straighten at the point of impact. It will also enable you to hit the ball with much more power.

(In the photo at right), the student has most of her weight on her front foot showing that she's transferred her weight forward as she hit. She could put even more power into her serve by taking a step into court with her back foot.)

COMPLETE THE FOLLOW-THROUGH

Until contact with the ball has been made, you are in complete control of a point because you've initiated the action. After you make your hit, you have to maintain a different kind of control—namely, control of your body. That's easily achieved if you follow through correctly.

When you finish the serve, you should have completed a more than 90-degree turn of your body from where you initially stood in your ready stance. Your chest should face the court to which you were serving.

So you should complete your delivery by bringing the racquet down across the body and around to the opposite side, taking a step into the court with your back foot to maintain your balance.

(In the photo to the left, the student has completed her follow-through with her racquet pointing behind her. She hasn't taken a step into the court because she's not yet ready to follow her serve to the net. Instead, she has all her weight on her front foot and is maintaining her balance with her back foot, ready to recover and stay behind the baseline to hit her opponent's return of serve.)

Serve/Checklist

1. Assume the ready stance and use a grip between the forehand and backhand grips.
2. Holding the ball lightly, release the ball so it rises in front of the baseline and to the inside of your forward foot.
3. Get your racquet into the backscratching position.
4. Move your weight forward as you reach up and out to make contact with the ball.
5. Keep your eyes on the ball throughout the serve.
6. Finish the follow-through.

THE SERVICE MOTION AT A GLANCE

The hit: Through proper timing and good body coordination, Seixas makes solid contact with the ball in this high-speed photo sequence.

MAKING PRACTICE FUN

GAMES YOU CAN PLAY

Many inexperienced players find tennis a frustrating game because they haven't yet acquired the skills to keep the ball in play for long. Too often, the serve is a fault or the return is netted and the points, as a result, are exasperatingly short. So in this chapter, we're going to suggest some ways you can improve your tennis and still have fun at the same time.

Most of these practice routines, though, can be used by better players, too. In fact, you can often work more effectively on specific parts of your game by practicing a stroke than by playing a practice match. So most of the following routines should be useful to any player.

WORK WITH A BACKBOARD

Whenever you have a few moments to spare, you can hit balls against a wall or a specially-built backboard. Stand well away from the wall and don't hit the ball too hard; you want to be able to return to the ready position after hitting the ball and yet have enough time to prepare properly for the next shot by taking your racquet all the way back. You can compete with yourself by seeing how many forehands you can hit in a row or how many alternating forehands and backhands.

USE A BALL MACHINE

When you want to work on a specific stroke, a ball machine will feed you balls endlessly and tirelessly (and without criticism, too). Get some advice on setting up the machine to get it to send balls to you fairly gently and with a decent interval between balls so you can recover after one shot and prepare properly for the next. Concentrate on making a full stroke and, then, on altering your direction so you can place balls to any part of the opposite court. Go easy at first since playing against a ball machine can be tough on your arm.

HAVE A FRIEND TOSS BALLS

If you don't have access to a ball machine, have a friend toss you balls to give you the same kind of practice on ground strokes. Ask your friend to throw the balls gently and consistently to the same spot until you begin to get your stroke grooved. If your partner has the skills, he can add more pace and length to his practice deliveries by hitting balls with his racquet or even getting into a mini-rally. It's best to have a bucket of practice balls for this routine so that you're not interrupted too often to pick up balls.

PRACTICING WITH OR WITHOUT A PARTNER

PLAY MINI-TENNIS FOR BALL-CONTROL

A practice game that will help you master ball control is a mini-version of tennis played inside the service boxes. To serve, the ball is dropped and hit (see right). so that it bounces inside the opposite service box. Play out the point just as you would a normal game of tennis; the only difference is that any ball bouncing outside the service box is out. Mini-tennis encourages controlled, gentle shots and lets you try angled placements of the ball.

DRILL IN A PRACTICE ALLEY

Many clubs, particularly those with indoor facilities, now have practice alleys where a player can work against a ball machine. The alleys take up less space than a regular court so more players can practice at the same time. Some practice alleys incorporate a backdrop with target areas (see left), which permits players to work on direction as well as stroke production. In a commercial club, practice time for an alley costs around $5 for a half hour. But it's well worth the expense for the concentrated practice.

BOUNCE AND CATCH A BALL

A simple way of improving your ball control is to bounce balls off your racquet, either up in the air or between your racquet and the ground. See how many bounces you can make without missing. When you become more skilled, you can vary the exercise by bouncing the ball on the ground and then catching it on the face of your racquet (see left). Catching the ball with your racquet will not only improve your hand-eye coordination; the knack also looks quite impressive when you are out playing a match.

RALLYING AND WORKING ON YOUR SERVE

DROP AND HIT TO SERVE
Beginning players often have difficulty developing adequate serves. It's painful to lose games by double faulting, but you can avoid that aggravation by beginning each point with a ground stroke. Start out with your racquet back at the end of the backswing and drop the ball with your other hand so that it bounces ahead and to the right (left for left-handers) of your front foot. You can then hit a forehand into the proper service court and to your opponent who should be in the normal receiver's position toward the back of his court. Then, play the point out in the normal way.

COUNT YOUR SHOTS AS YOU RALLY
If your game isn't quite good enough to serve and play in the normal way, or if you simply want to hone your ground strokes, you can practice competitively by hitting, say, forehands crosscourt to your partner counting the number of exchanges you make before committing an error. However, don't just loop the ball over the net. Concentrate on hitting the ball deep and using a full stroke. You can vary the pattern by hitting backhands crosscourt, for example, or by hitting backhands down the line to your partner's forehand.

SERVE WITH A BUCKET OF BALLS

The serve may be a difficult shot for novices, but it is, in a way, the easiest to practice. Just take a bucket of practice balls out on the court and hit as many serves as you can. Serving practice balls is an ideal way to experiment with your serve. If you think your ball release is too low, try placing the ball a little higher in the air. If you consistently hit your serve long, try placing the ball farther in front of your body; that will help you bring it down into the court. For even tougher practice, set up empty ball cans near each corner of the service box and see if you can knock them over with your serve. Keep a record of your performances when you practice and try to beat yourself every time you go out.

PRACTICE SERVES AND RETURNS

If you'd prefer some companionship when practicing your serve, enlist a practice partner. You can practice serving to him and he, in turn, can practice his returns of serve. But at the start, anyway, don't play out each ball as a point. That way, you can each concentrate on serving or returning serve without being concerned about winning the point. After serving a bucket of balls, you can collect the balls and change positions so you both have the opportunity to serve and receive. This type of practice allows the receiver to work on a specific return (such as down the line or crosscourt) and lets the server experiment with different placements to give the receiver a few problems. Of course, you can extend the practice by eventually playing points and then complete games.

STROKING/
PLATEAU
TWO

HOW TO PLAY THE NET

BE AGGRESSIVE

What's the main difference between the tennis novice and the intermediate player? The most obvious one is cleaner and more consistent strokes. The beginner is uncertain about hitting shots that the intermediate has had the time to work on and develop.

But there's another element, an intangible factor, that separates the two levels of play. It's called aggressiveness and it's acquired through the practice and repetition of shots that lead to confidence and, ultimately, greater mastery of the game.

Perhaps the most obvious sign that a player has this aggressiveness is an ability to get to the net and volley competently. When a player can do that, it means he or she can take command of a point and become the aggressor, putting an opponent on the defensive.

With this concept in mind, we move from the elementary stages of the game to the intermediate plateau. Here, the three ingredients of a sound net game are examined: Tony Trabert shows how to hit the approach shot, Ron Holmberg the forehand volley and Roy Emerson the backhand volley.

PLAYING THE SERVE-AND-VOLLEY GAME

One of the trademarks of an accomplished tennis player is his or her ability to play an attacking game in singles. Aggressive players are usually easy to spot on court because they frequently charge the net after each good serve and attempt to close out points quickly with well-placed, winning volleys. In approaching the net after a serve, you should be a couple of feet behind the service line when the receiver hits the ball. It's best to pause momentarily in order to determine the direction of the return and then move forward again toward the ball to hit your first volley.

GETTING TO THE NET

To take command of a point, you should get to the net as quickly as possible. Once there, a combination of crisp, clean volleys will usually win the point for you. To get to the net, you have to hit an approach shot. It's a simplified ground stroke that you hit when you're moving forward to intercept a ball that lands short in your court. The approach shot should be hit with enough pace and direction to allow you to move in quickly to your volleying position without fear of being caught in no-man's land between the service line and the baseline.

Since your momentum is already carrying you forward when you move in to hit the short ball, it's easy to follow your approach shot to the net. It's best to hit the approach shot deep and into a corner of your opponent's court. If you do that, you should be in a good position to finish the point because it will be difficult for your opponent to send a strong shot back at you.

KEYS TO THE APPROACH SHOT

SHORTEN YOUR BACKSWING

During a match, you should always be looking for opportunities to go to the net. Usually, these chances will come when your opponent makes a short return that bounces near the service line in your court.

When you see that the ball will land short, start moving forward to intercept it, bringing back your racquet as you run toward the net. Prepare for the shot as you would for a conventional ground stroke, as Trabert demonstrates above.

For the approach shot, though, the backswing should be shortened somewhat, because you won't have to hit the ball the full length of the court. Remember, too, that consistency and accuracy are more important than power with this shot. You should try to hit the ball deep to your opponent's weakness to set up a winning volley.

SIMPLIFY YOUR STROKE

Because there is often a lot of pressure when you advance toward the net, keep your stroking motion as simple as possible for the approach shot. In other words, don't try to be fancy.

When you move into the court, be sure that your body is turned sideways to the ball's line of flight (see photo above). Just before contact, start to transfer your weight forward and into the shot. If the ball your opponent hits stays low, bend your knees and get down to hit it with a smooth motion.

Remember, the approach shot should not be hit with the intention of winning a point outright. Just use your best stroke and place the ball well in your opponent's court. Of course, if your approach shot is a winner, so much the better.

When I see a short ball, my first move is into the court (frame 1). My racquet is already back (2) as I near the ball's line of flight. Transferring my weight forward, I start the racquet toward the ball (3). At contact, the ball is *about waist high, in front of my forward foot (4). During the follow-through, my racquet moves in the direction of the hit (5) and I continue toward the net, ready to volley (6).*

COMPLETE YOUR FOLLOW-THROUGH

For an approach shot to be successful, you've got to place it properly. If your opponent is playing deep and hits you a short ball, send your approach shot into the corner that's farthest away from him. If he's around the center line, go for his weaker side.

The secret of getting good placement and directional control on your approach shot is to follow through completely after you make contact. Keep the ball on the strings of your racquet for as long as possible and be sure the racquet head follows the line of flight of the ball.

The racquet head should finish well away from your body (see photo above). A complete follow-through will also turn your upper body to face the net. After the swing, your weight should be completely on your front foot, making it easy for you to continue toward the net.

COVER THE ANGLES

After you've completed your follow-through, you should have enough time to continue moving toward the net (see above) to intercept your opponent's return with a volley.

The best volleying position is about halfway between the service line and the net. Your feet should straddle the center service line. However, if your approach shot was hit deep to either corner of your opponent's court, you should move sideways a little, either left or right, to cover the possible angles or return. For instance, if you hit your approach shot into the left-side (or deuce) court, move slightly left of the center line.

By shifting to one side this way, you should find it easier to volley your opponent's return since you won't have to move quite so far to get to the ball.

KEYS TO THE FOREHAND VOLLEY

THE RIGHT GRIP

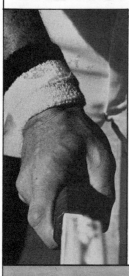

When you're at the net engaged in a rapid-fire exchange of volleys, you usually don't have time to change from a forehand to a backhand grip. So a Continental grip, halfway between the Eastern forehand and the Eastern backhand grips, should be used to hit volleys on both sides.

To arrive at the Continental grip from the Eastern forehand (or "shake-hands" grip), rotate your hand an eighth of a turn over the top of the racquet until the "V" formed by your thumb and forefinger is centered on the top panel of the handle (see photos).

PIVOT YOUR SHOULDERS

The backswing for the forehand volley is an abbreviated motion simply because you don't have the time to turn your body, step into the ball and follow through as you would for a normal ground stroke. So to get your racquet back, pivot your shoulders and upper body as soon as you see that the ball is coming to your forehand side.

By pivoting in this way, you'll discover that the racquet will swing back automatically with little arm motion. But keep the backswing short; the racquet head should not go any farther back than your rear shoulder.

If you have enough time, you should try to use your weight by stepping toward the ball which will add power to your shot.

My racquet is up, in front of me in the ready position (frame 1), with my weight forward. As I see the ball approach, I begin to pivot my shoulders (2), which automatically brings the racquet back as far as necessary (3). I step into the shot and make contact in front of my body (4). My swing is an abbreviated, punching-type of motion (5) and the follow-through is short to keep the volleying motion simple (6).

HIT OUT IN FRONT

As you step into the shot, you should make contact with the ball slightly in front of your forward foot, using a compact, slightly descending punching motion. If you hit out and forward properly with your weight behind the shot, the ball should safely clear the net and go down into your opponent's court.

At impact, the head of your racquet should be tilted back slightly. The racquet head should also be kept above the level of the gripping hand for volleys higher than the net to provide maximum leverage during the compact swing. Remember to keep your wrist firm and your grip tight at contact. That will help produce crisp, decisive volleys with good placement.

KEEP THE FOLLOW-THROUGH SHORT

The follow-through for the forehand volley is simply a continuation of the short, punching motion used in making contact with the ball (see above) rather than the extended follow-through of the normal ground strokes.

But even though the follow-through is brief, remember that it is a critical part of the stroke. You can't put the ball where you want it in your opponent's court unless you follow through in that direction. So after you hit a forehand volley, move the racquet forward with a sharp, jabbing motion along the line of flight of the ball.

The short follow-through is necessary because of the fast-paced action which often occurs at the net. It lets you recover quickly to prepare for your next volley.

KEYS TO THE BACKHAND VOLLEY

TAKE YOUR RACQUET BACK EARLY

As soon as you anticipate or see that your opponent's return is coming to your backhand side, pivot your upper body so that it is sideways to the line of flight of the ball. Keep your weight forward, on the balls of your feet.

This upper body turn, just the opposite of the pivot for the forehand volley, will automatically bring the racquet back as far as your rear shoulder. As you make the pivot, use your non-racquet hand to help guide the racquet back into the abbreviated backswing, as Emerson demonstrates above.

USE A FIRM WRIST

Just before you make contact with the ball, squeeze your racquet handle and your wrist will firm up as a result. A firm wrist is vital for control of a volley. If you have a loose wrist, the racquet will wobble at impact and severely hamper your ability to place the ball. Also, keep the head of the racquet above the level of your gripping hand to give you maximum leverage (see photo above).

If the return is wide to your backhand side, cross over with your front foot before you hit the ball. This step will give you valuable added reach on your volley.

When I see the ball coming to my backhand side, I start to pivot (frame 1), taking the racquet back with the help of my non-racquet hand (2). As the ball approaches, I step into the shot, bringing my racquet forward (3). I *make contact in front of my body (4), with my wrist firm. After the hit, my weight has completely transferred forward and into the shot (5). As with the forehand volley, my follow-through is short and simple (6).*

PUNCH THROUGH THE BALL

The forward swing for the backhand volley is, as it is on the forehand volley, a punching motion with a shorter follow-through than for a normal ground stroke. To help you maintain your balance during the shot, your stroking arm should move forward while the other one continues back in a spreading motion (see photo above).

Remember, too, to keep your eyes on the ball at all times. If you hit the ball out in front of your body and get down to the level of the ball when a shot is low, you'll find it easier to concentrate on watching the ball.

HOW TO HIT A LOB

WHEN AND WHY TO LOB

The serve, ground strokes and volleys—these are the basic shots that you must have to play tennis. But your shot repertoire will be incomplete—and your game will suffer for it—unless and until you can hit an effective lob. Why? Because of all the shots in tennis, the lob is the most versatile, the one shot that you can use with telling effect in both defensive and offensive situations.

Unfortunately, many weekend players almost never lob. They tend to think of the lob as a "sissy stroke"— an admission that they've been overpowered by an opponent, that they can't beat him with simple, straight-forward, bang-bang tennis. But that's a shortsighted view. In the pro ranks, for example, the best of the big-time players lob very well and whenever it might work to their advantage. And so should you.

The defensive lob is actually hit when your opponent has you out of position and on the run, either outside the sideline boundaries or deep behind the baseline. The shot itself follows a high, arcing trajectory (see diagram right) with the ball looping from baseline to baseline. The height and depth of a defensive lob buys you the time that you must have so that you can get back into proper position on the court.

The offensive lob, on the other hand, is generally hit from within your baseline when your opponent is hugging the net. Its trajectory, while not as high as that of a defensive lob, must be high enough to clear your opponent and his outstretched racquet. This type of lob can be especially effective when you're playing against an inveterate net-rusher. But it works well against anyone, and it's meant to be a winner.

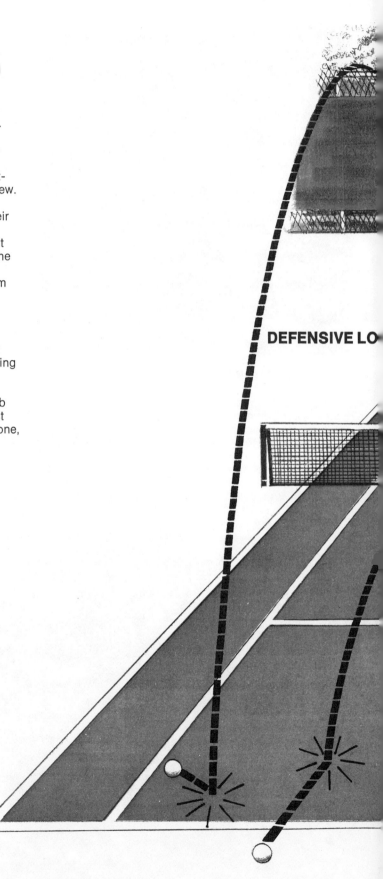

DEFENSIVE LO

OFFENSIVE LOB

KEYS TO THE DEFENSIVE LOB

SCRAMBLING FOR THE BALL

The first task in hitting the defensive lob is to get to the ball before it gets by you. That may sound like an oversimplification, but the only time that you should use this shot is when your opponent has hit a ball so wide or so deep that you have a great deal of difficulty in reaching it.

Wherever the ball goes, you should get to it as soon as possible. Use short steps, if you have the time, as you approach your intended point of contact. These smaller strides will help you to change direction, if necessary, and then to stop faster as you attempt to regain a more favorable court position.

Since you won't have much time to prepare for the shot, take your racquet back as you run to retrieve the ball. Also, force yourself to watch the ball all the way. It's difficult, naturally, to focus steadily on anything when you're scrambling as hard as you can. Remember, though, this is a shot that requires the utmost in skill and concentration, so keep your eyes on the ball!

TAKE A FULL BACKSWING

For a defensive lob to be effective, the ball has to be hit high and deep into your opponent's court. This means you'll want to use a long, flowing stroke with a full backswing and a complete follow-through. By taking your racquet back while you're running for the ball, you should be ready to start your forward swing as you reach the contact area.

That means you'll have to turn your body sideways to the line of flight of the ball, if possible, as you run. Don't try to disguise your swing. Draw the racquet back until it's pointing behind you, just as you would for a regular drive. If you shorten your backswing, you're inviting trouble because doing that will produce a weak shot that will pop up into the air and probably fall short. Your opponent will be waiting there with his mouth watering, ready to put the ball away. Taking a full backswing, though, will ensure a full stroke that will loft the ball high and deep into the opposite court.

HIT UP AND THROUGH THE BALL

If you examine the trajectory of the defensive lob (see pages 86-7), you can see that the ball has to travel farther through the air than a conventional ground stroke hit from baseline to baseline. So you should think of the defensive lob as a drive that must be hit high and deep in order for it to be successful.

To stroke the ball properly, bring your racquet up from beneath the line of flight of the approaching ball when you start your forward swing. At impact, imagine that you are driving the ball high into the air, making contact with the lower half of the ball and lofting it with a smooth, flowing stroke. Keep the ball on the strings for as long as possible to give you added control. You'll find this easier to do if you keep your wrist firm and your grip tight, just as you would for a normal stroke.

Don't try to add something extra to the shot by flicking your wrist at impact. Just hit through the ball upward and outward at impact, keeping your wrist firm.

FOLLOW THROUGH HIGH FOR DIRECTION

Hitting a ball high into the air is one thing. Placing it where you want it to go—a couple of feet inside your opponent's baseline—is quite another. One of the keys to doing that is a high, complete follow-through.

For maximum control over the height, depth and direction of the shot, you must first keep the ball on your strings for as long as possible and then follow through upward along the line of flight of the ball for as far as you can. At the end of your stroke, your racquet head should be high above your head in front of you. You can then use the time you've gained to get back into position and prepare yourself for your opponent's return.

One of the factors you should also take into consideration when hitting a defensive lob is whether there is any appreciable wind. Because the shot is so high, the ball will be easily affected by even the slightest breeze. So, if there's any sidewind at all, aim your lob down the center of the court to allow for a greater margin for error.

Since my opponent's shot has caught me out of position, I run for the ball taking my racquet back with a full swing while I'm moving to save time (frames 1 and 2). Keeping my wrist firm, I bring my racquet up to meet the ball (3). I open the racquet face before I make contact to lift the ball into the air (4). I follow through fully, with the racquet finishing high above my head (5) and I get back into position by using the extra time the lob has given me (6).

KEYS TO THE OFFENSIVE LOB

DISGUISE THE SHOT

The offensive lob is a surprise weapon that you can unleash whenever your opponent has dug himself in at the net and hits a shot that lands short. This kind of lob provides an alternative to the passing shot; you hit the ball over his head, rather than by him. Like the passing shot, though, it's meant to be a winner.

For the shot to be successful, you must catch your opponent by surprise. The best way to do that is to disguise your backswing—make it look as if you're getting ready to hit a ground stroke. That means taking a full backswing as you move in to meet the ball. Your opponent thus will have no way of knowing that you're about to loft the ball over his outstretched racquet.

The offensive lob calls for a lot of touch, the same as the defensive lob, but it's not a gentle stroke. You have to hit through the ball smoothly and solidly. And, again, remember to keep your eyes on the ball.

LIFT THE BALL

When you hit an offensive lob, you must be sure to stroke the ball firmly enough so that it loops high over the net, above and beyond the reach of your opponent. As with the defensive lob, that means keeping a firm wrist and a tight grip throughout the stroke. Otherwise, the best shot you're likely to produce is a weak floater.

The crucial factor in hitting the offensive lob comes, of course, at the instant of impact. The forward swing should be from low to high on a gently rising plane to give the ball enough lift to clear your opponent's racquet and land safely, deep near his baseline. The face of your racquet should be tilted back at impact so that it points a little toward the sky, but not as much as it would for a defensive lob. The strings should make contact on the lower half of the ball to help angle it upwards. But remember, don't incline the racquet face too much. If you do, the ball will sail too high and fall short, and then you'll really be in trouble.

As I move into the court to intercept a ball that has landed short (frame 1), I disguise my intention of hitting an offensive lob by taking a full backswing (2). I start my swing and bring the racquet forward (3). I make contact with the ball in front of my body with a slightly *open racquet face (4). After impact, my arms spread to help me maintain my balance (5) and the racquet continues up in a rising arc, following the flight of the departing ball (6).*

Defensive Lob/Checklist

1. Take your racquet back as you run for the ball.
2. Concentrate on the ball, not on your opponent.
3. Hit through the ball firmly from underneath.
4. Keep a firm wrist during the stroke.
5. Follow through high for better control.
6. Get back into position as fast as you can.

FOLLOW THROUGH COMPLETELY

To take full advantage of the offensive potential of the lob, you should follow through completely on the shot, just as you would with a defensive lob. That will ensure that the strings of your racquet remain in contact with the ball for as long as possible and so give you better control.

After you hit the ball, then, follow through as far as you can along the same path as the departing ball. And don't stop until your racquet is high overhead, pointing in the direction where you would like the ball to go. With luck —and a lot of practice—the ball will be up and over your opponent's head before he realizes what's happening.

You won't hit a winner every time, though, so follow up your shot by moving quickly to the net. It's also a good idea to aim your shot, if you can, toward your opponent's backhand. If he's forced to respond with a backhand overhead, one of the most difficult shots in tennis, you may still win the point even if your lob isn't quite perfect.

Offensive Lob/Checklist

1. Take a full backswing.
2. Watch the ball at all times.
3. Meet the lower half of the ball and hit through it.
4. Use a firm wrist and a tight grip.
5. Follow through completely.
6. Move in to the net.

HOW TO HIT AN OVERHEAD

For the intermediate or advanced player, probably the most satisfying —and most devastating—shot in tennis is a properly hit overhead. Why? Because no other stroke in the game offers as much offensive potential during a rally. It enables a skillful player to close out points quickly and convincingly, leaving opponents shaking their heads in frustration.

Remember, though, that the overhead—the normal reply to an opponent's lob—is not a simple stroke to execute. The shot is difficult to hit well because it demands careful body positioning and timing in order for it to be effective.

But the stroke is made somewhat easier by the fact that it shares many similarities with your conventional service motion. So the fear of hitting an overhead, which clouds the minds of many weekend players, is really unjustified. Because with patience, plenty of practice and the realization that placement is more vital than power in the shot, a reliable, effective overhead is within reach of most players.

On the following pages, Tony Trabert demonstrates the fundamentals of using the stroke in three situations: hitting the overhead after the ball bounces, on the fly and when you have to jump to reach the ball.

JUMP ONLY WHEN YOU MUST
Although it looks impressive, jumping to hit an overhead is often an unnecessary and sometimes costly tactic when employed by many weekend players. So unless you have to jump to reach the ball, hit all of your overheads with a flat swinging motion, keeping your feet on the ground. That allows you to transfer your weight forward properly and concentrate on timing the hit, whether you choose to take the ball after it bounces or on the fly.

But if the ball is out of reach, jump to gain as much height as possible, pushing off with your back foot and landing softly on the other. Also, remember to snap your wrist firmly, especially if you are forced to make contact with the ball behind you, in order to bring the ball down into the court and give you more power.

KEYS TO THE OVERHEAD

TURN SIDEWAYS TO THE NET

The overhead is your usual answer to a lob hit by your opponent. Whether it's a high, arcing defensive lob or a low, rolling offensive lob, your first move should be to turn sideways to the net (see photo above) and move back swiftly to the location on the court where you'll be able to meet the ball in front of your body.

That accomplishes two things: it helps you, first, to get into the proper sideways hitting position and, second, to get your weight centered on your back foot so that you can transfer it forward and into the shot. When you get into position, you should be standing about one foot to the side of the ball's line of flight. That will enable you to make contact with the ball above your hitting shoulder and not directly above your head.

SIMPLIFY YOUR MOTION

Although the stroking motions for both the overhead and serve are similar, there's one important difference: you prepare for the overhead by bringing your racquet up in front of you and then taking it back rather than swinging it down and back as with the serve. The reason? The compact backswing is quicker and makes it easier to time the hit.

So, lift the racquet up in front of your chest and then back, above head level, as you turn sideways to the net. Then, drop the racquet head behind you, keeping your elbow away from your side at about shoulder level. That will cock your wrist and allow you to get maximum leverage when you start your forward swing. As you bring back the racquet, use your other arm to follow the flight of the ball and maintain your balance.

Early preparation is a crucial factor in hitting a successful overhead. So as soon as I see that my opponent has hit a lob, I turn my body sideways to the net and begin taking my racquet up and back as I get into position (frame 1). Then, I plant my back foot and continue my backswing as my other arm follows the flight of the ball

and helps me maintain my balance (2 and 3). Now, with my wrist cocked and the racquet head down behind me (4), I'm ready to begin the forward stroke.
As I start the racquet upward, my weight begins to transfer off my rear foot (5). Through impact, my arm is fully extended and a strong wrist snap (6) accelerates

HIT OUT IN FRONT

One of the keys to hitting an effective overhead is to make contact with the ball just ahead and slightly to the right of your body (left if you're a left-hander). Position yourself behind the projected point of contact so that if you were to let the ball fall straight down from that point without hitting it, it would bounce on the court in front of your front foot. From there, you can transfer your weight forward and into the shot to generate added power.

As you swing up to meet the ball, rotate your shoulders forward and begin the weight transfer. Extend your arm fully as you near contact and uncock your wrist by snapping it through impact. This wrist snap provides power by accelerating the racquet head faster than normal. Try to hit the ball solidly and aim deep.

COMPLETE YOUR FOLLOW-THROUGH

After you've made contact with the ball, let the momentum that you've generated continue to take your racquet arm down and around your body so that the racquet ends up pointing behind you. This full follow-through should be identical to that of a hard flat serve.

If you cut your follow-through short, the racquet head will be decelerating through the impact zone. Completing the motion ensures that the head of the racquet will be moving at optimum speed when you meet the ball, and helps you transfer your weight forward during the hit. If you've followed through fully, you'll have to swing your rear foot forward in order to help you maintain your balance, since your weight will be moving toward the net. Recover into a good ready position.

Overhead/Checklist

1. Watch the ball throughout the stroke.
2. Turn sideways and retreat into position.
3. Get your racquet up and back early.
4. Make contact in front of your body with a strong wrist snap.
5. Jump only when you must.
6. Take a complete follow-through.

the racquet head through the point of contact. Notice that I keep my head up and never take my eyes off the ball during the entire stroke. After impact (7), my weight continues forward and my arm swings out and around my body in a complete follow-through with the racquet pointing behind me (8).

HOW TO MAKE YOUR SERVE A POTENT WEAPON

TWO BIG SERVES

A player who's moving up from the novice to the intermediate plateaus in tennis has to be able to do more on the serve than simply put the ball in play. It needs to be a more potent weapon.

So if you've mastered the basic flat serve, your next move should be to put some variety and sting into your delivery with the slice and twist (or roll) serves—two tough shots that can handcuff opponents.

They'll enhance your game in a couple of important ways. First, they'll enable you really to go on the offensive with your serve. And second, they'll make your deliveries more consistent since the spin that the slice and twist serves put on the ball gives it safer clearance over the net and helps to bring it down into the service box.

For example, the slice serve uses sidespin to make the ball curve into the court and then break to the right of the receiver (or to the left when a left-hander is serving). The twist serve combines topspin with a small amount of sidespin to make the ball kick high and a little to the receiver's left. This serve shouldn't be confused with the American twist serve because that requires an exaggerated stroking motion that should be attempted only by advanced players.

KEYS TO THE SLICE SERVE

CHANGE TO A BACKHAND GRIP

If, like most improving novice players, you use a flat serve, you'll have to change your grip for a good slice serve. It's best to use an Eastern backhand grip with the palm of your hand positioned on the top panel of the racquet handle. This grip will help you brush the racquet's face across the back of the ball.

One thing you should not change is your ball release. Use the same release that you would for your normal flat serve; that is, place the ball out in front of you so if it were allowed to drop, it would land about a foot into the court and to the right (if you're right-handed) of your front foot.

FLEX YOUR BODY FOR POWER

It's not necessary to be tall and muscular to hit a powerful serve. You can add power by putting your body weight into the shot as you hit the ball. Prepare by flexing your body and coiling it like a spring by bending your knees and arching your back slightly as you get your racquet into the backscratching position (see photo above).

Then, as you start your forward swing, uncoil your body by stretching upward. At contact, your body should be almost in a straight line as you lean forward into the shot. This uncoiling action will help you hit the ball higher in the air and put your body weight into the shot, making for a more powerful serve.

From my ready position, I drop the racquet head and my ball arm in unison to begin the ball release (frame 1). Then, with a smooth upward motion of my arm, I lift the ball gently, in as vertical a line as possible, out in front and just to the right of my body (2). As I'm doing that, I take the racquet up (3) and behind me into the backscratching position (4).

BRUSH THE BACK OF THE BALL

The key to the slice serve is to put sidespin on the ball by brushing the racquet head around the ball at contact. You should make contact at the back of the ball and continue that contact around to the side, or about the 3 o'clock position if you imagine that the back of the ball is surrounded by a clock dial.

You'll get more spin on the ball if you snap your wrist through the contact with the ball. That will accelerate your racquet head and, combined with your backhand grip, cause the racquet face to brush across the back of the ball and thus impart the necessary sidespin.

FINISH YOUR FOLLOW-THROUGH

After you hit the ball, the forward momentum that you generated by leaning into the shot and uncoiling your body should be enough to carry you at least one step into the court. As you take that step, finish your delivery by bringing the racquet around to the opposite side of your body in a complete follow-through.

If you find that your slice serves are weak and inconsistent, have someone watch your follow-through to ensure that you're not slowing down your racquet as you make contact with the ball. This extremely common serving error could be robbing you of the power and reliability that the slice serve offers you.

As the ball reaches the top of its flight, a little higher than the contact point, I swing my racquet up and forward (5), keeping its head laid back and my wrist cocked. Just before impact, I snap my wrist forward (6),

making contact with a brushing motion to put spin on the ball. I continue into my follow-through (7) and finish with the racquet behind me (8).

KEYS TO THE TWIST SERVE

USE A MODIFIED BALL RELEASE

For the twist serve, you should use a Continental grip. That's reached by rotating your hand one-eighth of a turn over the top of the racquet from the standard Eastern ("shake-hands") forehand grip. The Continental grip will position the racquet face at the proper angle to put spin on the ball.

Lift the ball more to the left (right if you're a left-hander) than for the slice serve. It should rise above your left shoulder so that if you were to let the ball drop without hitting it, it would strike the baseline. Also, don't place the ball quite as high as you do for the slice serve because your contact point should be a bit lower.

ARCH YOUR BACK FOR SOLID CONTACT

If you've placed the ball correctly on the release, the next part of the service motion should come almost automatically. Since the ball has risen above your front shoulder, the only way you'll be able to make solid contact is to get your weight well back and move the tennis racquet up and over the ball.

To prepare for that kind of a swing, you must arch your back more than you would for a slice serve to give you the leverage that's needed to apply the desired twist to the ball.

So as you bring the racquet behind you, transfer your weight onto your rear foot by arching your back and flexing your knees.

HIT UP AND OVER THE BALL

With your body coiled like a spring, bring the racquet straight up behind your head in a smooth swing, keeping your wrist cocked. As you do that, you should begin shifting your weight forward and onto your front foot.

Then, just before impact, snap your wrist sharply so that the racquet face hits the ball in an upward brushing motion.

If you were to imagine a clock dial around the back of the ball, you should make contact at a point just past the 6 o'clock position and then hit up and over the ball to between the 12 and 1 o'clock positions. The wrist snap is vital in order to put the heavy topspin and slight sidespin on the ball.

FOLLOW THROUGH TO THE SIDE

After you make contact with the ball using the sweeping, upward stroking motion, you must let the racquet continue out and away from your body to make sure that you've hit through the ball completely and imparted the proper amount of twist or spin. The twist service motion will push the racquet farther out to your right (for right-handers) than your normal slice and flat serves because there is much less forward movement involved in the swing.

From this position, finish your follow-through naturally by taking a step into the court and letting your racquet head come down by your side.

The initial motion for the twist, or roll, serve (frame 1) should be nearly identical to the one used for the flat and slice serves. The major difference occurs when I release the ball (2) because I have to place it closer to my body to impart the proper spin. Of course, during the release, my other arm continues to take the racquet back (3) until its head is well down behind me (4)—a point from which I can begin the forward swing.

As you can see, I arch my back throughout the motion, since the ball is almost directly above me. I begin the forward swing by bringing my racquet arm up with my wrist cocked. Then, to put the required combination of topspin and sidespin on the serve, I bring the racquet head up and over the ball with a pronounced snap (5 and 6) and finish the stroke with the racquet head down by my side (7 and 8).

WHEN TO SLICE...WHEN TO TWIST

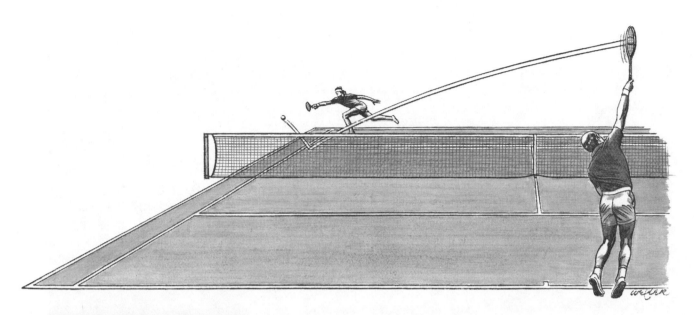

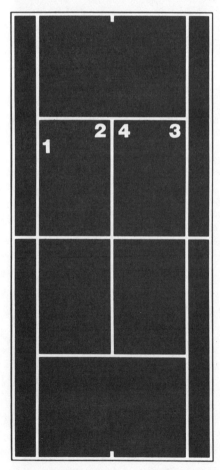

HOW TO USE THE SLICE SERVE

If you've ever had the misfortune of being on the receiving end of an excellent slice serve, you can fully appreciate the shot's effectiveness. From the receiver's viewpoint, a right-hander's ball curves to the right in the air as it crosses the net, lands in the service box, and then breaks away from you, to your right after it bounces. (The break is to the left on a left-hander's slice serve.)

Now that you possess the skills to hit this serve, how are you going to use it? Should you hit it on the first or second serve? Actually, it doesn't really matter. The slice serve is slower than the flat serve and the sidespin helps to pull it down into your opponent's service box. So it's an excellent percentage serve. But it's also a great change-of-pace delivery if you've been hitting flat serves during a match and you want to catch your opponent by surprise with the deceptive slice.

Next, where should you place the slice serve? For simplicity's sake, let's refer to the court diagram on the left and assume both you and your opponent are right-handed. Your best move when serving into the deuce court (the one to your left) is to hit the ball shallow and wide

(position 1). That should pull your opponent out of court and allow you to move in toward the net where you can volley his return back to the right into an open court. Or you can aim the ball toward the center line (2) where it will curve sharply into his body and, you hope, handcuff him.

You can achieve the same effect when serving to the other side, the ad court, by going wide (3) in hopes of jamming the receiver. Hit the ball deep and down the middle (4) only if you think you'll catch your opponent sleeping because he'll be in a good position if he manages to make a return.

Slice Serve/ Checklist

1. Use a backhand grip.
2. Flex your body as you drop your racquet head behind your back.
3. Watch the ball at all times.
4. Snap your wrist to brush the back of the ball.
5. Follow through across your body.

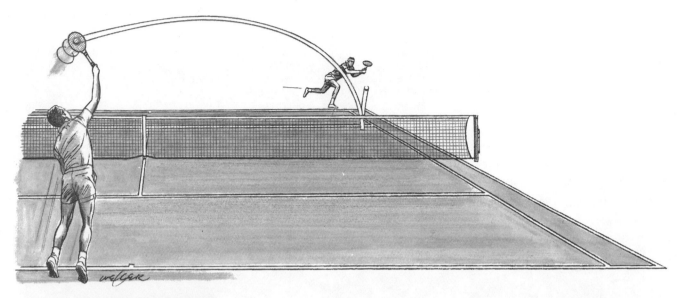

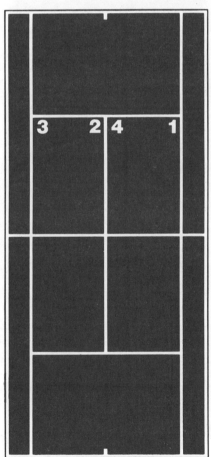

HOW TO USE THE TWIST SERVE

The twist serve's combination of heavy topspin with a touch of side-spin makes it a tough shot to return with any power for most club-level players. The spin gives you two advantages. First, it allows you a greater margin for error by bringing the ball down into the service box much more abruptly than your slice serve (which uses only sidespin) and your flat serve. And second, the spin causes the ball to kick shoulder-high and slightly to the left of the receiver (to the right on a lefty's serve), a position from which it's difficult to make a powerful return.

In other words, the spin makes the twist serve a high percentage shot and transforms it into a valuable weapon at the same time. It's prob-ably best used as your second serve since you're almost always certain to get the ball into play. Its troublesome, high kick will also give your oppo-nents problems when they try to over-power the relatively slow-moving ball. Once in a while, though, it's a good idea to lead off with the twist serve just to keep your opponents honest. And if you have a good slice serve, the offensive potential of the twist is substantially increased.

Remember to serve the ball deep into your opponent's service box. A short twist serve will allow him to come in and pick off the high bounc-ing shot easily. Assuming you're both right-handers, your first option is to hit the ball into the corner when serving to the ad court (position 1 in the diagram at the left) because the ball will kick about shoulder-high and tend to pull him away from the center of the court. By serving deep and down the middle in the deuce court (2), you may force him to hit a weak, high, backhand return that you can put away. To make the ball kick into his body, place the ball at the other locations (3 and 4).

Twist Serve/ Checklist

1. Use a Continental grip.
2. Release the ball above your front shoulder.
3. Arch your back and get the racquet head down behind you.
4. Snap your wrist to brush upwards on the back of the ball.
5. Follow through down by your side.

HOW TO STRENGTHEN YOUR GROUND STROKES

START FROM THE BASICS
As your game improves, you're probably finding that you'd like to do more with the ball. You can play respectably well. Now, you'd like to upgrade your ground strokes, for instance, by adding spin for variety.

Before you take that step, though, remember that you must have a solid foundation to build on; you must have mastered the fundamentals of sound stroking before you begin experimenting with spin. Even the top professional players, when they're experiencing problems with a forehand or backhand stroke, will go right back to the basics to find out what's wrong.

This chapter on improving your ground strokes starts with Stan Smith demonstrating how you can put some topspin on your forehand while Julie Anthony schools you in the slice, or underspin backhand.

KEYS TO THE TOPSPIN FOREHAND

HIT UP TOWARD THE BALL

To develop a good topspin ground stroke, you need only make small adjustments to your present forehand or backhand. Do not attempt to imitate the excessive topspin strokes of a Guillermo Vilas or a Bjorn Borg. Those strokes require a precise timing and racquet control that takes years to develop.

Begin by positioning your racquet lower at the end of your backswing than you normally do. That way, it will be below the anticipated contact point and you'll be able to swing forward on a rising plane to meet the ball. This action will produce extra topspin with very little modification of your stroke.

There is no need to alter your grip or to change the angle of the face of your racquet at contact. But you may have to bend your knees a little more to make sure that you swing up to meet the ball.

MAKE SOLID CONTACT

It's the upward motion of the racquet face at contact that puts the topspin on your ground strokes. However, you should not merely attempt to brush the back of the ball in order to impart topspin. You must also hit through the ball as you would with a conventional ground stroke. In fact, you can hit the ball as hard as you like because the topspin will help bring the ball down in your opponent's court. The harder you hit the ball, the more topspin you will generate—provided that your racquet is moving up and through the ball.

Keep your racquet face perpendicular to the line of the ball, as Smith is doing here. If you try to roll your wrist in an attempt to add even more topspin to your shot, you'll probably hit the ball into the net. Leave the roll to Rod Laver and his exceptionally strong wrist.

Just as I do for a normal forehand, I prepare early (frame 1) with my usual backswing (2). But the racquet head is lower at the start of the forward swing (3). I swing forward and up to meet the ball (4), making firm contact in front of my body (5).

USE AN UPWARD FOLLOW-THROUGH

One significant difference from the flat forehand comes right after contact. Don't follow through out in the direction of the ball as you do on that stroke. If you do, you'll add little spin to the ball.

Instead, let the racquet face continue moving upward on pretty much the same plane that it's been following since you began the forward swing. Don't force the racquet up with an exaggerated motion. It's not a violent stroke, remember, so keep it smooth and flowing. There shouldn't be any sudden motions of your arm or racquet.

As you develop confidence in your topspin forehand, you can steepen the angle of your forward swing. But do it gradually so you can measure the effect the change is having on your shots.

FINISH HIGH IN FRONT

If you hit your topspin forehand correctly, your racquet should finish higher than it does on a flat stroke. In fact, as Smith shows above, your racquet face will be almost vertical to the ground and you'll be looking over your shoulder at the departing ball. The precise position of the racquet head does not matter—as long as you finish high. That high follow-through will mean that your racquet has been moving up correctly as you hit the ball.

The same principles apply to the topspin backhand. You should prepare with the racquet lower, swing forward on a rising plane, hit through the ball with a racquet that is moving up and forward, and complete your follow-through with a high finish. You'll find that even small adjustments to your stroke can provide significant amounts of topspin, provided that you hit through the ball.

The racquet continues upward after contact (6) but the face is still almost vertical to the ground (7) and not rolled over. My racquet then finishes high in the air and in front of my body (8) and my weight is almost entirely on my front foot.

KEYS TO THE SLICE BACKHAND

PREPARE WITH YOUR RACQUET HIGH

Since underspin, or slice, is the opposite of topspin, the nature of the swing is reversed for underspin shots. Instead of swinging from low to high, you must swing from high to low to impart underspin. So you should prepare with your racquet higher than the ball at the end of your backswing. Use your other hand to take the racquet back, as Anthony demonstrates above, because that will help you keep the racquet head up.

The backhand is particularly suited to the sliced shot because of the mechanics of the backswing on that side; it's easy to get the racquet in a position to swing from high to low. That's much tougher to do on the forehand side. So you're better off slicing your backhand.

You can slice almost any ball but remember that the slice backhand will have less power than a flat or topspin shot.

SWING ON A DOWNWARD PATH

Although a sliced ball doesn't have the momentum (or "pace") of a topspin shot, you must still meet the ball solidly and put your weight into the stroke to give some power. So step toward the ball as you swing forward in order to get your weight moving into the shot. Your racquet should be moving on a downward sloping path. Don't make it too sharp an angle, especially at first; simply modify your normal backhand swing slightly.

Think in terms of driving the ball, just as you do with your regular backhand, because the shot should go deep into your opponent's court.

Remind yourself, too, to keep your eyes fixed on the ball. The underspin shot calls for control and, to get that, you must hit the ball near the center of your strings. So watch the ball intently in order to meet it as close to that spot as possible.

As soon as I decide to hit a backhand, I take my racquet back (frame 1) until it is higher than the flight of the oncoming ball (2). I then swing forward and slightly down (3) so that the racquet is moving on an inclined plane toward the ball (4). I make contact in front of my body (5) with my racquet continuing to follow the ball after it leaves my racquet (6). This racquet motion continues into the follow-through (7) and I finish the stroke with my racquet well out in front (8).

HIT FIRMLY THROUGH THE BALL

When you make contact with the ball, drive through it firmly. You are not trying to undercut the ball as you might in hitting a drop shot. You should hit the ball relatively deep into the other court. However, a sliced ball will tend to float and slow down more than a normal backhand, so you should hit the ball hard and put your weight into the shot.

Meet the ball in front of your body with a firm wrist and grip and with your arm almost straight—as Anthony is doing here. You will find that you have to tilt the racquet face back a bit to get the ball to clear the net by a safe margin. Don't tilt the face too much, though, or you'll hit a weak floater that may prove an easy set-up for your opponent.

Keep your racquet moving downward and forward through the contact with the ball.

USE A STRAIGHT FOLLOW-THROUGH

The natural tendency when hitting a backhand is to finish high. But on the underspin shot, you should follow through straight out after the ball to make sure that you don't pull your racquet up during contact. So just let the racquet head follow the direction of the departing ball for as long as possible. You can then let the racquet arm come up naturally.

As with topspin ground strokes, you should experiment with the slice backhand to find the most comfortable and effective swing for you. You'll discover it's a versatile stroke that will help you hit both deep and short when necessary. But don't overuse this or any other spin shot in your repertoire. Spin is a refinement that you can add to your ground strokes to make them more potent. But if spin doesn't work for you, remember to go back to the basics of the ground strokes.

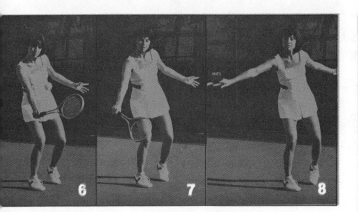

Topspin Forehand/ Checklist

1. Concentrate on the ball.
2. Get your racquet back early.
3. Swing forward on a rising plane.
4. Keep your racquet face perpendicular to the ball's line of flight.
5. Hit through the ball and finish with a high follow through.

Slice Backhand/ Checklist

1. Take your racquet back higher than the projected contact point with the ball.
2. Swing from high to low on a descending plane.
3. Hit through the ball.
4. Follow through in the direction of the shot.

SHAPING UP FOR BETTER TENNIS

Let's face it. Physical conditioning is a turn-off for many people, including tennis players. They recognize they should spend more time warming up and getting in shape in order to play their best. Like reading the classics or washing the windows, they know it would be a good idea. But it's too much like work and not enough like fun. So they put it off.

If that's more or less the case with you, look at it purely from the standpoint of self-interest. If you fail to get and to stay reasonably fit, you'll never come close to realizing your potential on court or to enjoying the sport as much as you could. On the contrary, you'll be leaving yourself vulnerable to ailments and injuries that will detract from your game, at best, and will keep you from playing, at worst.

It's not especially hard to develop and adhere to a balanced exercise routine. Essentially, you should divide your exercise routine into two parts: (1) a pre-match warm-up that consists mainly of stretching exercises you can do on the court; and (2) an off-court program encompassing a variety of exercises that will increase your stamina, flexibility and muscle strength.

If you question your ability to do any of the exercises described in this chapter, consult with your physician before you attempt them.

PRE-MATCH WARM-UPS: GETTING LOOSE

A painful muscle tear or hamstring pull that keeps you rooted to the sideline for a couple of weeks is a heavy price to pay for carelessly neglecting to loosen up properly before playing a match—especially since that warm-up takes only a few minutes of your time.

So while you're waiting for a court to open up, you should take a few minutes to limber up the muscles in your arms, legs and back to prepare them for the demands you'll make of them when you step on the court and begin play. You can do that easily by performing a few stretching exercises such as the ones shown here. After your warm-up, your body will be flexible and you'll be able to move more freely to get to the ball.

Be aware, though, that the exercises demonstrated here will not in themselves build your stamina or improve your muscle strength overnight. Indeed, for your body to get the most out of a warm-up session, the exercises should be augmented by a regular off-court conditioning program.

ACHILLES TENDON STRETCH
You can use the net to stretch your Achilles tendons—those vital cords of body tissue that connect your calf muscles to your heels—and prevent painful injuries. First, place one foot ahead of you and reach out to grasp the top of the net, as Julie Anthony is doing. With your other foot placed comfortably as far behind you as possible, flex that rear leg at the knee, keeping your heel and entire foot in contact with the ground. Don't bounce; stretch the tendon gently. Stay in that position for about 10 seconds and then repeat with the other leg.

You can also use much the same technique to stretch your calf muscles. Just keep your back leg straight at the knee and move your upper body toward the net.

LEG AND BACK STRETCH

The muscles in your legs and back take a lot of punishment on court, so it's important that you loosen them up sufficiently before you play. For the exercise that Tony Trabert is demonstrating above, begin by standing with your feet spread as far apart as you comfortably can. From this position, reach down with both hands to touch your right foot, then straighten up and follow the same procedure to touch your left foot. Repeat the exercise about 10 times. If you can't touch your feet at first, don't worry. It may take a couple of stretches to limber up your muscles enough to reach down that far.

WIND SPRINTS

Tennis is a game requiring short, sudden bursts of speed. So to prepare yourself for them, you should limber up with a few wind sprints before a match—as Roy Emerson is doing here. Run the length of the court along the sideline as quickly as you can two or three times. It will loosen up your legs, expand your lungs and get your blood flowing quickly. If you do some wind sprints each time you warm up, moreover, your agility and stamina are bound to improve.

ARM AND SHOULDER ROTATION

To loosen up your arm and shoulder muscles, stand with your feet about shoulder-width apart and extend your arms so that they're parallel with the ground. Then, as Vic Seixas shows above, begin rotating your arms forward at the shoulders so that your hands draw small circles in the air. Gradually increase the size of the circles, and finally, reduce them to get your arms and hands back into their starting positions. After completing this cycle, start again, this time rotating your arms in the other direction.

OFF-COURT CONDITIONING: GETTING IN SHAPE

Do you run out of gas in the third sets of your matches? Do your muscles often ache the day after you play? Then you're probably neglecting to exercise properly off court. Even players in top condition need to follow a good exercise routine between matches in order to build up muscles and to tone them for peak performances on the tennis court.

The exercises demonstrated on these two pages are designed to improve your overall performance on the court in three important ways.

Try to stick conscientiously to this off-court exercise program and combine it with a wise use of your pre-match warm-up time. By doing that, you'll not only reduce the risk of suffering an injury but increase the amount of enjoyment you get out of playing tennis, too.

FOR STRENGTH...

SIT-UP
For building up the stomach and back muscles, few exercises can equal the good old familiar sit-up. If it's done regularly as part of your off-court program, this exercise can work wonders for your strokes—particularly the serve. To begin, lie down with your knees bent and your soles on the ground. Clasping your hands behind your head, sit up and touch your left knee with your right elbow, as Vic Seixas demonstrates below. (Anchor your feet under something like a low sofa or have someone hold them down the way Julie Anthony is doing for Seixas.) Lie back and then sit up again, this time touching your right knee with your left elbow. Do five to 10 alternating sit-ups at first, and gradually increase the number of repetitions as your back and stomach muscles strengthen.

SUPERVISED PROGRAM
One of the quickest ways to develop your muscles for tennis is to follow a body-building program at a health club. In the photo above, Billie Jean King is shown working out on an exercise machine that's designed to tone and build up specific muscles in the body. Of course, programs using such machines should be supervised strictly by knowledgeable personnel because if the machines are used improperly, they can do you more harm than good.

FOR FLEXIBILITY...

BACK STRETCH

The muscles in your back need to be in shape because they're instrumental in helping you to reach every ball and to stroke all your shots fluidly. To improve their flexibility and performance, try the exercise shown on the left by Tony Trabert. First, lie flat on your back with your arms extended along your sides and your palms planted on the ground. Swing your legs up and over so that they're pointed over your head parallel to the ground. You should feel your back muscles stretch. After holding this position for about 20 seconds, return to the starting position and repeat the exercise several times.

THE V-UP

This exercise is another designed to flex the muscles in your back. But it strengthens your leg muscles, too. Start from a sitting position with your legs stretched out and your hands down at your sides. Bring your knees up slowly, as close to your chest as possible. At the same time, stretch your arms out in front of you, as Ron Holmberg is doing on the right. Repeat the procedure as often as you can. When the V-up becomes easy to do, you can make it harder by starting from a prone position.

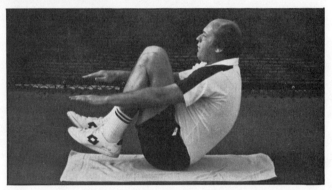

FOR STAMINA...

JUMPING ROPE

Remember the days when you used to jump rope as a child? Back then you did it because it was fun, but now you can use the same exercise to increase your stamina and build your leg muscles—particularly in the calf areas. It will also condition you to stay on the balls of your feet, one of the prerequisites to good footwork on court. Start by jumping for a couple of minutes per day and then, like Julie Anthony, try to build that time up to five minutes or more.

JOGGING

The astounding popularity of this form of exercise in recent years is ample testimony to its many benefits. For the tennis player, there is probably no better way to develop the stamina and leg strength that are needed on court. It improves your circulation and helps you to breathe more efficiently under physical stress. So set aside a certain time each day for jogging. Start slowly and try to work up to two or three miles a day—moving at a brisk but comfortable pace. If you can, stay off asphalt or concrete surfaces since they can be punishing to the joints in your legs.

SINGLES: HOW TO PLAY
THE SERVE AND VOLLEY GAME

BEYOND STROKING

There's a lot more to playing successful tennis than simply being able to hit the ball across the net. For example, unlike golf—where everything depends on the mechanics of stroking—tennis adds a crucial and challenging variable: the player on the other side of the net.

His or her presence over there means that you've got to have more going for you than good strokes if you hope to win. You must know where—not just how—to hit the ball.

You must develop the ability to vary that placement depending on the opponent and the conditions. You must learn when to sit back and stroke drives from the baseline, when to lob, when to take the net to volley. You must, in short, acquire a command of tennis strategy.

The classic proof of the importance of strategy often comes in those age versus youth matches. A veteran player faces a young hotshot who's

faster, stronger and at least his equal in stroking ability. Yet the veteran will win much of the time. And the reason, invariably, is a keener knowledge of strategy gained through years of match experience.

So once you've developed consistent strokes, the next step is to learn how to put those strokes to their best use. This chapter is the first of three designed to acquaint you with the basic strategies of singles competition. It tells you how to play the serve-and-volley game.

KEYS TO AN EFFECTIVE SERVE

STAND NEAR THE CENTER MARK

Nearly everyone who plays tennis can quickly tell you that the proper serving position in singles is behind the baseline, close to the center mark. But you'd be surprised to find that not too many of them really understand why that's the most effective position from which to serve. Do you?

First, you can cover the entire court for the receiver's return more efficiently from this position. If you stand nearer the singles sideline, as you normally do in doubles, you open up the other half of your court to a down-the-line return that you have less chance of reaching. Serving near the center mark also gives you the shortest distance to run to hit your first volley.

Just as important, this position gives you a wider choice of service placement. In serving to the deuce (left-side court), for example, you can force the receiver wide with a slice serve or make him hit a backhand with a flat or twist serve down the middle. From the serving position used in doubles, though, you virtually telegraph your intentions of hitting a slice serve wide to your opponent, since that's usually the best serve you can make given the angles you have available.

And finally, your opponent will have less time to read the serve when you start near the center mark, because the ball won't be in the air as long as it would be if you were to serve near the sideline.

GET YOUR FIRST SERVE IN

A strong, reliable first serve is the foundation of a serve-and-volley game. Without it, your opponent can tee off on the ball. And you'll be watching a lot of shots whiz by you as you advance to the net to attempt a first volley.

But having that strong first serve doesn't mean that you have to pull out all the stops and unleash a screaming cannonball. Too many club players have that mistaken impression and try to hit a "gorilla" first serve. The results are plenty of double faults, lost service games and frustration.

Instead, go out on a practice court and experiment with your first serve by using slightly less pace. Slowing your serve down just a little by adding some spin will work miracles for your accuracy—to say nothing of those disastrous scores. When you reach a point where you can get at least 65 per cent of your first serves deep in the service box, let the amount of pace you used be your upper limit most of the time. Of course, if you've got a good, hard first serve and get it in play consistently well, use it to your advantage. But don't let it become a habit.

Above all, remember that most points in tennis are lost on errors, not on placements. So a consistent serve with good speed, if it's directed at a player's weakness, will produce more points in the form of errors than your erratic cannonball serve ever could.

WHERE TO PLACE YOUR FIRST SERVE

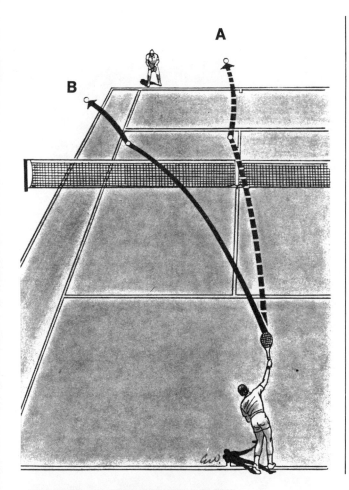

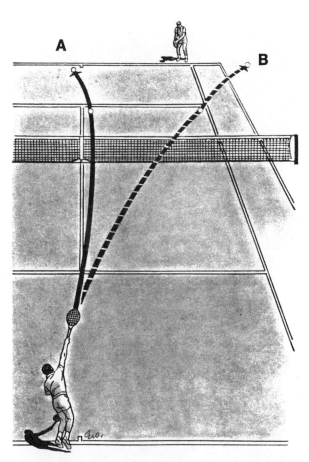

SERVING TO THE DEUCE COURT

Before deciding where to place the ball on your first serve, you've got to determine where your opponent's weakness lies. And the most effective way to do that, especially when you're playing someone for the first time, is to watch him closely in the pre-match warm-up to see which of his shots is weaker.

At the club level, you will usually find the weakness on the player's backhand side. So when serving to the deuce court, one of your best options is to hit a serve deep down the middle (A in the diagram above) to force your opponent to make a backhand return (assuming that he's a right-hander). He will not only have to take the ball on his weak side, he'll make contact near the center of his baseline, reducing his possible angles of return and increasing your chances of volleying well off of his shot.

A good alternative is to hit a slice serve three or four feet in from the corner of the service box that will force him wide of the court (B). That will give him a wider angle to return. But if he's not accurate enough to send the ball down the line and into the corner, he'll have to drive it crosscourt. And you'll then be able to volley it back to your right into his open court.

Don't try to hit your first serve to the same spot every time. Mix things up and keep your opponent off balance.

SERVING TO THE AD COURT

You should have the same basic objectives in mind when you hit your first serve to the ad court as you do in serving to the deuce court. That is, you usually want to serve the ball away from your opponent, preferably to his weak side and, occasionally, directly at him.

But there's one important difference that you should recognize. Let's say you hit a flat or slice serve down the middle to the ad court (A in the diagram above). With that placement, you're sending your opponent scrambling for the ball, to be sure, and cutting down his angle of return. But you're also hitting it to his strong forehand side (if he's right-handed) and he'll end up in fine position, near the center of the baseline, to defend his half of the court.

Now, contrast this situation with the one you created when you served a slice into the corner of the deuce court. There, the serve forced your opponent wide and opened up the entire court.

You can achieve the same result in the ad court by serving a few feet in from the corner of the service box (B). You're hitting to your opponent's normally weaker backhand side. And the serve will force him away from the center of the court. The chances are that he won't attempt the risky down-the-line shot. Instead, he'll probably try to angle it crosscourt where you can pick it off.

WHEN TO GO TO THE NET

DECIDE BEFORE YOU SERVE

Advancing to the net after you hit your first serve puts a lot of pressure on your opponent. He has to be more accurate with his return since a good first volley on your part will put you in a commanding position at the net to hit a winning second volley.

But your decision to move in behind your first serve is one that must be made before you hit the ball. If you stay back near your baseline and wait to see where your serve bounces before you decide to come in, you'll get caught in no-man's-land between the baseline and the service line. And you'll be faced with hitting a tough volley or half-volley at your feet.

If you hit your first serve deep into a corner, that will allow you enough time to get close to the service line before the ball comes back at you. So don't hesitate after your serve. And remember to release the ball out in front of your body; that way, you have to lean forward to hit the ball and your follow-through should automatically take you into the court—a position from which it's easy to continue forward.

Move to the net on a diagonal path, following the direction of your serve. For example, if you serve wide to the deuce court, advance to the point slightly to the left of the center line. That will permit you to cover angles of return. But, get to the service line quickly.

THE TIMES TO STAY BACK

A serve-and-volley offense can produce lots of points and even enable you to blow an opponent off the court at times. But you should be aware that the strategy can also backfire on you in certain cases.

So there will be times when you should be ready to abandon your attacking style, at least temporarily. One of those situations occurs whenever you're playing on a clay court, because that surface slows the ball down and gives your opponent a better chance to make the kind of return you can't handle en route to the net. Another time to stay back is when you're facing a player with an exceptionally strong return of serve.

Remember, though, your decision to stay back must be made before you serve. After you make contact with the ball on your serve, take a natural step into the court on your follow-through and then retreat immediately behind the baseline. You'll still have plenty of time to prepare for your opponent's return.

Two other obvious cases which require a more conservative style of play are when either your serve or volleys go sour. So when you get passed a few times on the return of serve or when you lose confidence in your net play, stay at the baseline. Who knows, maybe in a few games you'll get your strokes grooved again so that you can go back on the attack.

PLAYING TO WIN AT THE NET

HIT YOUR FIRST VOLLEY DEEP

Your first volley, hit from the vicinity of the inverted "T" formed by the intersection of the center and service lines, will rarely be an outright winner because your opponent in most cases will be able to reach the ball. The shot's principal function is to permit you to advance closer to the net where you can knock off a more effective second volley and, you hope, win the point.

To hit an effective first volley, pause momentarily as you approach the service line to determine the direction of your opponent's return just as the ball is hit. Then move forward again to meet the ball. You should concentrate on hitting a firm volley (but not necessarily an overpowering one) deep into the corner of the court farthest away from your opponent (see the diagram above).

By placing the ball in that spot, you'll force him to make a shot on the run. Ideally, he'll have to hit up on the ball to clear the net and that's the easiest shot for you to volley away for a winner. Of course, you must be careful. If your first volley lands short, your opponent will be able to move in on the shot and drive it past you.

Finally, don't remain at your service line after you hit the ball to see where it lands. Advance even closer to the net into your normal volleying position with your racquet held in the ready position prepared to hit your next volley.

PUNCH THE BALL ON YOUR SECOND VOLLEY

Once you've forced your opponent back into a corner with your solid, first volley, your next step should be to assume an aggressive volleying position about halfway between the service line and the net. To cut down your opponent's possible angles of return, stand to the same side of the center line where you hit your first volley. From that position, you should have a good chance to reach any rising ball as it crosses the net.

Your plan of action for the second volley should be simply to punch the ball back across the net, shallow and sharply angled into the service box that's away from your opponent (see the diagram above). Usually, this sequence of volleys—the first one deep and low to the corner and the next shallow to the other side—will be enough to win the point from most opponents. But even if you're up against a player who runs like a gazelle and can reach your second volley, it should be a relatively simple matter to firmly block back his return to the open half of the court.

Once in a while you may also encounter an opponent who seems to have ESP and anticipates the direction of your putaway volleys with astonishing prescience. Your strategy in this case should be to hit behind the player to try to catch him on the wrong foot as he runs to the spot where he thinks you're going to hit the volley.

EXPLOITING THE SECOND SERVE

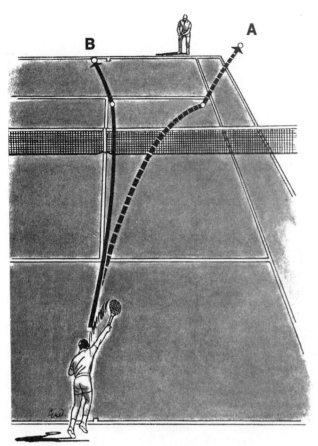

USE SPIN TO MOVE YOUR OPPONENT AROUND

The offensive potential of the second serve is rarely
exploited by most club-level players. Instead, they tend
to concentrate on developing an overpowering first serve.
As a result, their second serves suffer and often become
soft, flat marshmallows that any competent receiver can
handle with ease.

Now's the time particularly to use the slice and twist
serves. Both are reliable, yet deceptive because of
their spin.

Hit slightly short of the corner in the deuce court, a
slice serve will pull the receiver wide beyond the sideline
where he'll probably try to return crosscourt rather than
attempt the lower percentage down-the-line shot. A twist
serve hit down the middle into the deuce court will
bounce high and to a right-hander's backhand, a difficult
position from which to generate any power.

The twist is also highly effective when served deep into
the corner of the ad court (A in the diagram above). It
will kick wide and force your opponent to hit that high
troublesome backhand again. A slice serve deep down
the middle will draw the receiver in toward the center of
his baseline (B).

When you become proficient at placing your second
serves, experiment with trying to make the ball kick or
slice into the receiver's body. That will give many players
fits because they won't know which way the ball is going
to bounce.

WAIT FOR A SHORT BALL TO MOVE IN

Although many advanced players have the ability to
charge the net behind their second serves, it's usually
wiser to remain at your baseline and wait until your
opponent hits a short ball before you try to move in
toward the net.

The reason is fairly simple: unless you hit the ball with
enough depth and spin, your opponent will be able to
move in on your serve and fire a return you'll have
trouble handling.

So your best bet is to stay back initially and rally
aggressively. After you hit the serve and take your step
into the court, get back behind your baseline. Try to
move your opponent around with ground strokes. And
when he hits a short ball, don't hesitate. Move in on it,
hit an approach shot and get to the net.

However, there's no reason to stay back after your
second serve if you're serving the ball consistently deep
and with accuracy—especially if you're fooling your
opponent with your slice and twist deliveries. Take
advantage of that situation by moving in just as you
would after a first serve. The extra time it takes for slice
and twist serves to cross the net should give you an
opportunity to close in on the net quickly enough. And a
good spin serve might even force your opponent to hit a
weak floater that you'll be able to volley away easily for
a winner.

THE LEFT-HANDED GAME

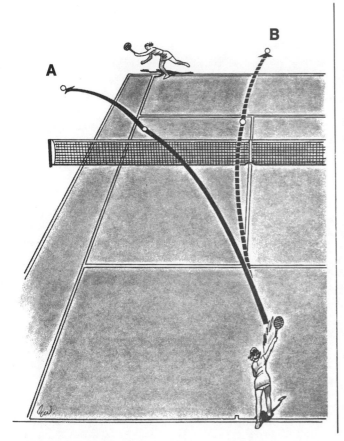

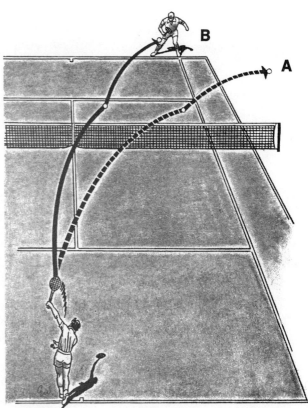

SERVING TO A LEFTY

It's probably happened to you at least once since you began playing tennis. You play four or five games of a match before you realize that your opponent is a lefty! That means that every shot you thought you hit to his weakness, actually may have gone to his strength.

How do you serve to a left-hander? First, knowing that your opponent is a lefty, think things over carefully before you serve that first ball. Get it clear in your mind that if you want to serve to his weakness, you'll have to place the ball into the opposite side of the service box from where you would normally serve to a righty.

So in facing a lefty in the deuce court, your best weapon will be a slice serve wide to the corner (A in the diagram above). That will force him into the alley and make him hit a backhand as he's scrambling for the ball. Advance to the net behind this serve, and then volley his return into the open court. Unless you're trying to catch him off-guard, avoid a flat serve down the middle (B) since he'll take it on his forehand side and be in great defensive position afterward.

To the ad court, hit a slice serve down the middle to his backhand. A twist serve into the other corner could mean trouble if he's strong enough to power it down the line with a high forehand. But always vary your serves to keep him honest.

SERVING IF YOU'RE A LEFTY

The left-hander gets his revenge on the tennis court for the sly discrimination he suffers in a right-handed world. For once, he has the advantage.

If you're a lefty, you can cash in first on that advantage with your serve. All your deliveries will break the other way from those the receiver is used to seeing when he faces a right-hander. So to capitalize on this edge, you should concentrate on using your spin serves to move your opponent around and keep him guessing.

Your most damaging serve will be the slice, especially on the second serve. When serving to the ad court, you have two effective placements for the slice. Your best bet is to hit it near the sideline, a couple of feet in from the corner, to force your opponent wide of the court to his backhand side (A in the diagram above). For variety, aim the slice serve down the middle (B). The ball will break sharply into the receiver's body and will probably make him hit it with a cramped forehand stroke.

You have two similar placements in the deuce court. Hitting a slice deep near the sideline will make the ball curve into your opponent's body. Your other option, of course, is to aim it down the middle which will force him to hit a backhand since the ball is breaking away from him.

SINGLES: HOW TO WIN FROM THE BASELINE

A MORE CONSERVATIVE GAME PLAN

To win consistently, all players must develop a command of backcourt strategy. That's true even for compulsive net-rushers who prefer the serve-and-volley game. They'll have to play from the baseline many times after second serves or when they're playing on a slow surface that discourages net play.

There's much more to good baseline strategy than simply staying back and trading ground strokes with your opponent until one of you makes an error. You may occasionally win with that kind of defensive approach, of course. But you've got to know how to move your opponent around on the court, for example, and when to take advantage of a short return to move in to the net. To do that, you have to temper your aggressiveness with patience and wait for the first opportunity to take the offensive.

This chapter describes how you can most effectively return serve, wear down an opponent from the baseline, and eventually assume an offensive position at the net.

USING THE RETURN OF SERVE

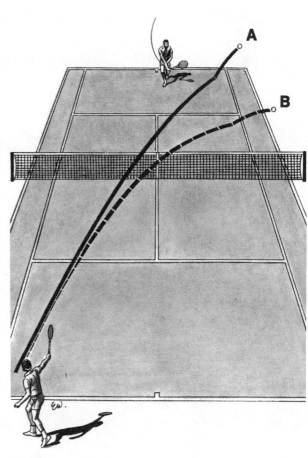

PLAN YOUR RETURN STRATEGY

There are very few situations in tennis, especially at the intermediate level and higher, where you're able to win matches using defensive tactics alone. To improve your chances of success, you must always be on the lookout for opportunities during points that will let you gain the offensive and put pressure on your opponent.

Don't concede anything to the server, for example, when you're the receiver. Even before he starts his service motion, you should have a specific plan in mind about where you're going to try to place the ball so that you can blunt his offensive edge. That task is made easier if you can detect a definite serving pattern.

This advance planning is vital because there isn't enough time to make a placement decision in the split-second that it takes for the ball to reach you—especially if you're facing a strong server. Too many players don't plan and, as a result, make sloppy returns because they hit the ball on impulse. So the key to returning serve is to plan ahead and stay loose and relaxed yet alert in your ready stance where you normally stand to receive serve.

WHERE TO PLACE YOUR RETURN

Unless you're lucky or extremely good, your chances of hitting service returns for outright winners consistently are very slim. So it's foolhardy for you always to try to slam the ball back with that purpose in mind.

Instead, concentrate on making solid contact and placing the ball in a position from which it will be difficult for your opponent to attack with his shot. A good rule to follow when the server does not rush the net is to return deep crosscourt (A in the diagram above) because that will give you the biggest area of court to hit into.

If your opponent's serve is weak, return down the line occasionally to catch him off guard. And don't take unnecessary risks. Aim your return a few feet in from the corner and use only as much power as you can easily control.

When your opponent follows his serve to the net, a good option is to hit a shallow shot into his court (B), preferably with some topspin. He won't be able to get much power into his shot so he'll have to hit the ball up in order for it to clear the net.

DUELING FROM THE BASELINE

AIM FOR ACCURACY AND DEPTH

To play successfully from the baseline, you've got to keep your opponent at or behind his baseline. You want to prevent him from getting up to the net where he can dominate the point. To do that, you must consistently hit your ground strokes with good depth and accuracy.

These two qualities should form the nucleus of your baseline game. They allow you to rally offensively, yet defend your half of the court effectively from your position at the baseline.

Depth is crucial because it forces your opponent to stay back and rally. As a result, his returns from the baseline will be in the air longer and you'll have more time to react. That way, he won't be able to advance to the net and assume a good volleying position. Accuracy, too, plays a big part in the baseline game because, with it, you can keep an opponent on the move and prevent him from getting into a groove.

Of course, playing from the backcourt also puts you in excellent defensive position. The chance is slim that you'll be victimized by an outright winner from your opponent.

MANIPULATE YOUR OPPONENT ON COURT

Essentially, there are two types of baseline players: one who's content to trade ground strokes monotonously with an opponent until a mistake is made, and one who can rally purposefully from the baseline, skillfully maneuvering an opponent around until he can seize an opportunity to charge the net.

The second style is, obviously, going to take you a lot further in the game. And the key to it is to learn to vary the placement of your ground strokes in your opponent's court. In singles, shots hit deep crosscourt and into the corner away from your opponent (A in the diagram) achieve that for you. They also test the stamina of the other player. And if you're able to detect a flaw in your opponent's game, exploit that weakness by directing your shots there often during a match.

Avoid falling into a predictable pattern with your drives, though. Try to keep opponents off balance by mixing things up a bit. One way to do that is to hit behind your opponent (B) if he or she guesses that you're going to hit the ball to another spot on the court and begins running there.

DEALING WITH A NET RUSHER

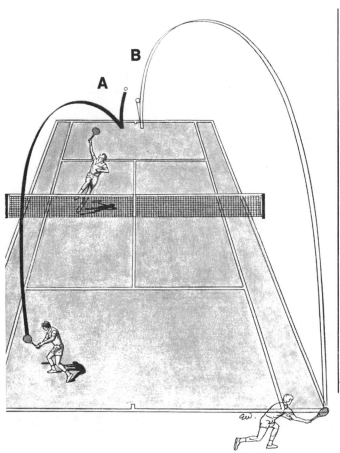

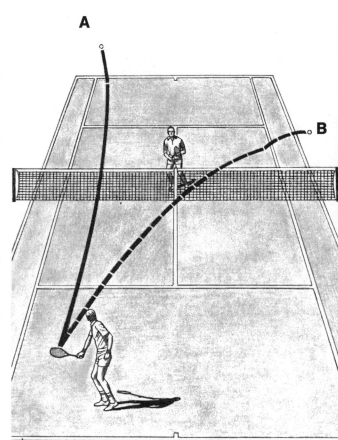

LOB OVER AN OPPONENT

Try as you might, there will be times during a match when you offer up a short, weak ball that your opponent can jump on and use to gain the net. When that happens, one way to nullify his advantage is to employ the lob—either the low-flying offensive lob (A in the diagram above) or the high, arcing defensive lob (B).

That will back him away from the net. And if he doesn't have a strong overhead with which to return a lob, you may be able to gain the net yourself or even win the point outright. In any case, the simple knowledge that you can lob may discourage an opponent from taking the net as much as he'd like. Or if he does charge in, he probably won't crowd the net where he can volley more easily. And he may overplay his volleys, trying to place them too precisely so you won't be able to loft another lob over him. A judicious use of the lob, in short, will give the net-rusher real pause.

After you hit a successful offensive lob, be ready to advance to the net yourself. Most players don't have the ability to retreat and return this lob with any power. So you may get an opportunity to attack on his return and take charge of the point in your forecourt.

HIT PASSING SHOTS TO THE SIDE

After you hit a few effective lobs against a net-rusher, you've got him thinking about backpedaling and having to hit an overhead each time he comes to the net.

So the mere threat of your lob gives you an opportunity to introduce the other major weapon that you have at your disposal when he comes to the net: the passing shot.

One alternative for passing an opponent who's camped out in his forecourt is to aim your shot down the sideline (A in the diagram above). If the ball is sharply hit, the net-rusher will have trouble reaching it from his volleying position near the center line where he stationed himself to cut off your possible angles of return.

If you've forced your opponent back from the net a bit with your lobs, then try using a passing shot that's angled so it travels crosscourt and lands shallow in his court (B). He'll have difficulty reaching it. This shot isn't an easy one, though; it's best suited to advanced players because it requires a delicate touch to hit the ball so that it eludes the net player but still lands in bounds.

PLAYING THE WAITING GAME

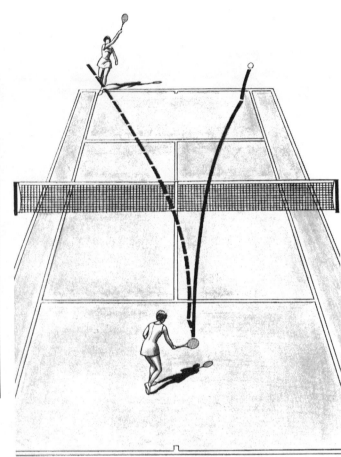

PUT THE PERCENTAGES TO WORK FOR YOU

One of the traits that often separates the successful baseline player from the unsuccessful one is his ability to play percentage tennis. He rarely gambles during points by taking foolhardy risks with low percentage shots that can backfire on him. Instead, he concentrates on each shot as it's hit and doesn't think too far ahead about moving in to the net until a good opportunity presents itself.

This talent isn't easy to acquire. It requires a great deal of patience and the ability to keep cool under pressure during play. These qualities are essential in playing a backcourt game because, many times, you've got to persevere through seemingly endless baseline rallies, all the while keeping alert to capitalize on every opportunity that might give you an edge. If you allow yourself to become overanxious during points, then you'll probably rush your swings and start overhitting your shots with disastrous results.

So when you're playing back, wait patiently for your chance to take the net. If you consistently hit your shots deep, your opponent won't be able to attack and you might even force him to gamble with a low-percentage shot.

CAPITALIZE ON A SHORT RETURN

The patience and consistency that you put to good use during long rallies will often have their reward in the form of short returns hit by your opponent. When that happens, stay calm but jump at the chance to take command of the point.

Move in on the short ball as it bounces close to your service line and stroke an approach shot deep into the corner away from your opponent—preferably to his or her weakness (see the diagram above). Occasionally, hit your approach shot directly at the opposing player; that will cut down the angles he has available to hit a passing shot by you as you move to the net. After you make contact with the ball, continue forward and get into your volleying position, about halfway between the net and service line. Be prepared to punch back the return.

If you play another baseliner who patiently retrieves your shots and lobs over you when you take the net, change your strategy sometimes as you move in for a short ball. Instead of hitting your approach shot deep, angle a short return or even hit a drop shot to force your opponent to run in toward the net. Doing that can really pay dividends if he has a fear of playing the net.

SINGLES: HOW TO CLOSE OUT A POINT AT THE NET

GETTING AN EDGE

Once you've learned the basics of service strategy and developed a solid baseline game, it's time to take the next major step toward becoming a respected, all-court player: acquiring a working knowledge of the tactics you can use at the net to close out points quickly and decisively.

That involves far more than stroking fundamentals. You must know how to cover the angles on attempted passing shots, where to place your volleys for maximum effect, how to "read" and react to your opponents' movements on court and where to direct your overheads. A familiarity with these subtleties of the game, and the ability to execute each of them well, can give you the edge you need against many opponents—especially those who like to camp on their baseline. That's because your proximity to the net opens up more of your opponent's forecourt as a target for your shots.

Your presence at the net also puts a great deal of pressure on the other player. If you can play smartly and confidently from your volleying position, you'll probably force him or her to make errors by attempting to hit risky, low-percentage shots past you.

So it's to your advantage to incorporate the net strategies outlined on the following pages into your overall game plan.

THE KEY FUNDAMENTALS

COVER THE ANGLES

Winning tennis matches with consistency depends a great deal on your ability to cover your opponent's possible angles of return on each shot. And although that principle applies to your play in every area of the court, it takes on added importance when you're volleying at the net.

The reason is simple: shots reach you faster when you're in the forecourt, so you don't have enough time to run after balls hit wide. That's why it's important to position yourself so that you can reach the ball and cut off your opponent's options with a minimum of body motion. In the diagram above, the near player is correctly following an approach shot to the net. By moving in along the arrow, she will bisect her opponent's angle of return and be in good position to reach both shots.

So whether you're making your initial move to the net behind a solid serve or approach shot, or attacking at the net in the middle of a point, take up a volleying position about halfway between the net and service line. Stand slightly to the side of the center line where you hit your last shot. Covering the angles in this way will enable you to reach more shots.

MAKE YOUR OPPONENT HIT UP

Of course, your ultimate goal in assuming an offensive position at the net is to take command of a point and close it out quickly, preferably with a well-placed volley that your opponent won't be able to touch with his racquet. But it's not necessary to hit outright winners all the time in order to play a capable net game.

On the contrary, strategically placed volleys—ones that make your opponent dash around his backcourt and move him from sideline to sideline—can be just as productive as the clean winners. That's especially true in the later stages of a match when he begins to wilt from all of the running he's been doing.

The key to making this tactic pay off for you is to force your opponent to hit up on the ball, as Vic Seixas is doing in the sketch above, so that it's rising when it crosses the net. You can often force this type of return by keeping your volleys low to the ground and away from your opponent. Then, when the ball arrives, it's simply a matter of ending the point with a firm volley that you should be able to angle away cleanly into an open area of the court.

PLACING YOUR VOLLEYS

PUT HIGH VOLLEYS AWAY

When you succeed in forcing your opponent to hit rising, defensive shots, you should be in an excellent position in your forecourt to make contact with the ball above the level of the net—a height from which you'll be able to inflict the most damage with solid volleys. That's because your proximity to the net will allow you to volley the ball down into your opponent's court and angle it more sharply toward a sideline.

To put away high volleys consistently, you should have a definite target in mind before you make contact. When you're able to meet the ball above the net, there are three target areas you should consider: areas A and B are near the sidelines and are relatively shallow. That means you can angle the ball into them to make your opponent cover a large area of the court.

Area C is located directly behind your opponent and should be used to keep him honest or catch him going the wrong way if he anticipates a volley to the sideline. Whichever targets you select in a rally, avoid falling into a pattern with your volleys or your opponent may capitalize on your predictability.

SEND LOW VOLLEYS DEEP

Not every ball that you'll want to volley will come to you in your forecourt at a point tantalizingly above the level of the net where you can put it away crisply and decisively. Your opponent will be doing his best to drive passing shots by you or, the next best thing, hit balls at your feet that will force you to get down and volley up so the ball clears the net safely.

When you're faced with making these low shots, it's crucial to keep your composure and avoid trying to do too much with your volleys. You won't be able to hit the ball as firmly as you can on a high volley because too much power will usually send it sailing beyond your opponent's baseline. And if you try to angle it shallow near his service line, your softer shot will often be an easy set-up for him to drive back for a winner.

So in hitting a low volley, you should try to place it deep near your opponent's baseline, usually into the corner that's farthest away from him—indicated by the target areas in the diagram above. If your low volley is placed properly, he won't be able to attack it and you'll have plenty of time to recover at the net and set up for your next volley.

PARRYING THE PASSING SHOT

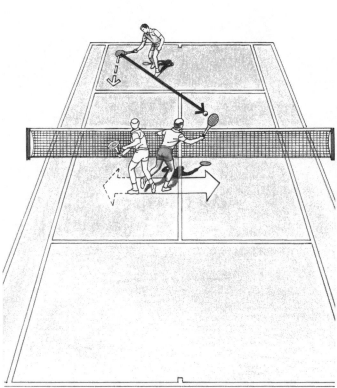

HOW TO ANTICIPATE PASSING SHOTS

Each time you advance to the net during a match, you claim an offensive advantage over an opponent. But you give yourself even more of an edge if you're able to anticipate to which side of you he'll direct his attempted passing shots.

The key to doing that is to observe him closely and try to detect patterns in his play during your match. For example, if he hits most of his passing shots crosscourt, play the percentages and shift your position slightly to cover that side more effectively. The chances are he feels more confident hitting a crosscourt shot and will go back to it often in pressure situations.

But what should you do when you face a player who mixes his passing shots well? Look for specific clues in the way he sets up for each hit that could tip off the direction of his passing shot. Usually, the most telling sign is the way a player aligns his body and feet before impact, as Stan Smith demonstrates above. If he takes a slightly open stance (right), it's likely he'll go crosscourt with the passing shot. And if he lines up more squarely to the ball (left), he'll probably hit down the line.

FEINT WHEN IN TROUBLE

How many times have you gone to the net with visions of put-away volleys in your head, only to mis-hit the stroke and dump a soft, shallow shot your opponent moves in on and slams back at you across the net? You seem to be helpless. What can you do?

Perhaps your best option is to try to fake out your opponent and entice him to hit the ball where you can reach it. That may sound difficult, but it's actually fairly easy to do. All that's required is a simple, but convincing, head fake or a false step—not a lot of jumping around—toward one of the alleys to make your opponent think that you're moving to cover that side of the court just as he's starting his forward swing (see the diagram above). That will invite him to hit to the side you seem to be opening up.

Once you've made your fake, though, reverse direction. If you're lucky and your fake was good enough, you may have fooled him completely. By the time he realizes he's been tricked, it will be too late for him to change the direction of his shot and you'll be able to reach the ball and capture a point that you otherwise would have lost.

REBUFFING THE LOB

WHEN TO EXPECT LOBS

To relieve the offensive pressure that you're generating at the net, your opponent will frequently rely on lobs to gain temporary reprieves from your aggressive volleying forays. As a result, you should be prepared to retreat toward your own baseline to run down the ball and return it with an overhead or drive. So your ability to anticipate your opponent's lobs, like his passing shots, will pay quick dividends.

Of course, the obvious time to expect a high defensive lob is when you've got your opponent on the run and out of position behind the baseline (demonstrated by Julie Anthony in the top sketch). Remember, it's a defensive shot so it won't be disguised by your opponent. The two telltale signs to look for in anticipating the shot are a pronounced upward swing of the racquet and a racquet face that's pointing toward the sky.

The low offensive lob is much more difficult to antici- pate because it can be disguised well. With this lob, your opponent is in control, usually moving in to hit the shot off of a short ball with an upward swing and slightly open racquet face as Julie Anthony demonstrates in the bottom sketch.

WHERE TO HIT OVERHEADS

When your opponent sends up a defensive lob in response to your net attack, he's admitting that you've gotten the best of him with your crisp volleys. And if his lob isn't deep enough, then you can end the point quickly with a powerful, well-placed overhead.

The three targets you should aim for when you hit an overhead are almost the same as the ones you use for your volleys. When your opponent's lob falls inside your service line, try for a clean winner by hitting deep and into one of the corners of his court (areas A and B above). Of course, to keep your opponent honest, it's a good idea to occasionally smash a ball behind him (area C). When a lob lands deep, though, nearer your base- line, be content to send an overhead or a drive off the bounce solidly to his weaker side. It's tough to hit the corners of the court from that distance.

And finally, to return a quick, deep offensive lob that you know you can't reach with an overhead, scramble back for the ball quickly and loft a defensive lob in reply because the chances are your opponent will be moving to the net behind his shot to attack.

DOUBLES: HOW TO SERVE EFFECTIVELY

THE THINKING MAN'S GAME

There's a saying in pro tennis that spectators buy tickets to see the singles—but stay to watch the doubles.

Doubles, thus, is too often an over-looked form of the game, one that's not fully appreciated for the drama and sophisticated skills it involves until it's properly exposed. At the pro level, unfortunately, it all too seldom gets this kind of exposure (how often do you see doubles on TV, for example?).

But at the club level, doubles play is bourgeoning today for a number of reasons: 1) it's less taxing physically than singles; 2) it's an excellent vehicle for socializing; and 3) it gets twice as many players on a court as singles, a crucial consideration given the increasing demands for court time in the aftermath of the tennis boom.

Doubles, though, is not just singles to the second power. The presence of another player on each side of the net, plus a court that's bigger by a third, changes the dynamics of play in subtle and significant ways. So to play doubles successfully requires an understanding of a different kind of strategy and an ability to synchro-nize on-court movements with a partner.

It all starts with the serve, of course, where some important accommodations have to be made. So this chapter, the first of three on doubles play, outlines the correct tactics and movements of the server in match situations.

SERVING BASICS IN DOUBLES

WHERE TO STAND

To serve effectively in doubles, you should always try to keep your opponent guessing and prevent them from expecting a particular serve. So you should assume a serving position that will give you the widest variety of placement options. The ideal position is just behind the baseline, about halfway between the singles sideline and center mark, as Julie Anthony shows you on the right.

This central position is best for several reasons. First, it allows you to serve over a lower part of the net into both corners of each service court.

Of course, serving straight at your opponent is possible, too. Second, you're squarely in the middle of the area you have to cover for the return. And finally, if you decide to rush the net, you can advance straight in along the shortest path to the net to make your first volley.

Your partner at the net, meanwhile, should be about halfway between the service line and the net, standing a little closer to the singles sideline than to the center line. That way, he should be able to cover the alley or the middle of the court by moving one step in either direction.

TAKE SOME SPEED OFF YOUR FIRST SERVE

While every club player dreams of acing opponents with a lethal, cannonball first serve, it's best to lay aside such fantasies in doubles. On the contrary, a more consistent serve hit at three-quarters speed with good depth and spin is a more effective weapon. The slower serve not only puts the ball into play more reliably, but also gives you more time to advance to the net and prepare to hit a first volley.

The slice serve, demonstrated by Billie Jean King on the left, should be used most of the time. You can hit the ball hard, but the spin on it will help bring the ball down into the service court faster. The twist serve is also effective, especially on the second serve and on a slow court. Don't gamble with your power serve unless you're very consistent with it or way ahead in a match.

The ability to put your first serves into play consistently also puts a lot of pressure on a receiver. He will be forced to respect your first serve and stay back behind his baseline to make the return.

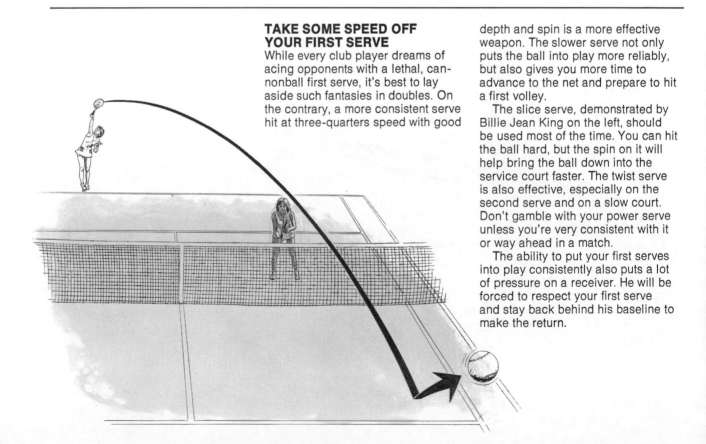

PLACING YOUR FIRST SERVE

INTO THE DEUCE COURT

Depth is the most important factor in putting the ball into play. If you hit a shallow serve, the receiver can charge the ball and pound a shot at your feet as you advance to the net or perhaps he can even hit an out-right winner. At the very least, he'll be able to assume an offensive position in his forecourt.

As in singles play, you should direct most of your first serves to your opponent's weakness and, at the club level, that's usually the backhand side. So assuming the receiver's a right-hander, your most productive serve into the deuce (left side) court will be a spin serve down the middle (A in the diagram). Unless the receiver is able to return the ball at your feet, the chances are that you or your partner will get a shot that you can volley solidly.

Your other alternative is to hit a slice serve wide to the receiver's forehand (B). Be careful, though. Unless the forehand is his weaker stroke, he may be able to send the ball down the line or angle it sharply crosscourt, pulling you into the alley and opening up your court for a volley return down the middle. Of course, an occasional serve hit directly at your opponent can be tough to return, too.

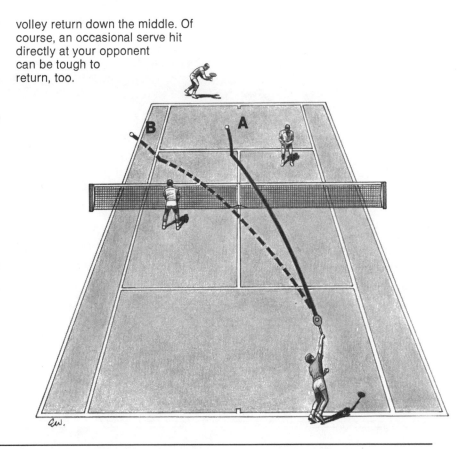

INTO THE AD COURT

You should carefully weigh your opponent's strengths, weaknesses, and ability to anticipate your serves when you decide where to place the ball in the ad (right side) court.

If the backhand is the weak link in a right-handed receiver's game, you should aim for the backhand side, a few feet in from the corner of the service court (A in the diagram). A spin serve placed to the backhand accomplishes three things.

First, the serve pulls him away from the center of the court. That opens a gap between the receiver and his partner where you can attack with your first volley. Next, since your serve is traveling diagonally across the net, the ball will be in the air longer and allow you to move closer to the net. And finally, the receiver will probably try to go crosscourt with the return rather than attempt a risky down-the-line shot, so your partner may get an opportunity to poach and pick it off for a winner.

A slice serve down the middle (B) can also be an effective weapon. Although the serve will go to the receiver's forehand side, it will draw him into the center of the court and reduce his possible angles of return.

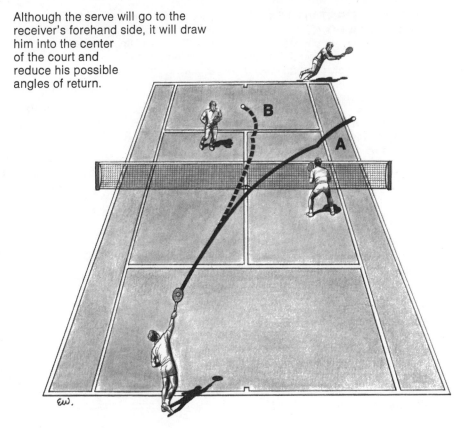

TAKING THE OFFENSIVE AT THE NET

FOLLOWING YOUR SERVE

To win consistently in doubles, you must almost always follow your serve to the net and help your partner put pressure on your opponents. Otherwise, your team will be in the awkward and intrinsically weak position of having one man up and one man back—a situation that your opponents will try to exploit.

You should follow your serve in the same way that you would using a singles serve-and-volley strategy with one important exception: instead of running in diagonally along the direction of your serve, advance straight forward toward the middle of your half of the court, as Billie Jean King demonstrates.

Just as the receiver is about to make contact with the ball, pause by making a small, hopscotch-like straddle facing the net. Stay on the balls of your feet to see where his return is headed and then change direction to meet the ball.

Remember, though, to run in after every serve. Don't wait at the baseline to see if your serve is good. If you do, and a serve you think will be long falls into the service court, you'll probably get caught too deep in no-man's land and be faced with the prospect of making a difficult half volley.

USE YOUR FIRST VOLLEY TO SET UP A POINT

In doubles play, the chances are that your opponent will often be able to manage some sort of a return. And most likely, the receiver will hit crosscourt to you as you advance to the net, since that return gives him the most court to work with and, thus, greater margin for error.

That's why you should be in a good position, just behind your service line or even closer to the net, if possible, to intercept his return and volley it back.

Your first volley should not be an attempt to hit a winner since you'll be too far from the net to hit down effectively. Instead, your first volley should be a setup shot designed to keep your opponents away from the net so they can't do much damage. For your first volley, concentrate on meeting the ball squarely and sending it back deep if the receiver stays back, or low near his feet if he's following his return toward the net (see diagram on the right).

If he's advancing, a successful first volley will force him to bend down for the low ball and hit a weak shot that's rising as it crosses the net. Then, it's simply a matter of volleying the ball down and away from your opponents for a winner.

ew.

WINNING WITH YOUR SECOND SERVE

TRY THE TWIST SERVE

Spin serves are tailor-made for doubles play. Although the slice serve is generally the most powerful spin delivery, the twist serve, too, packs a punch of its own because it kicks up sharply and, as a result, keeps opponents in check near their baseline. In addition, the twist's reliability makes it a particularly effective weapon when used as a second serve.

One of the biggest advantages that the twist serve gives you is the length of time that the ball remains in the air before it makes its steep nosedive into the service court. Because it has a higher arc than the flat and slice serves, the twist gives you a precious second or two extra to move even closer to the net before you hit your first volley.

What's more, the high, kicking bounce of the twist serve makes it difficult for the receiver to hit the ball with much power, especially if you direct it to a right-hander's backhand —down the middle to the deuce court or into the corner of the ad court (see A in the diagram).

As an alternative, you can also send the twist serve down the middle to the ad court (B) where the ball will then kick into the receiver's body. That placement will cut down his angles of return, too.

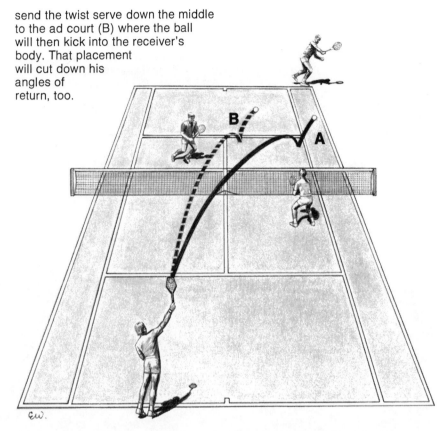

REMEMBER THE AUSTRALIAN FORMATION

In doubles play, you'll occasionally encounter a team of players who possess an uncanny knack of being able to return your serves so low crosscourt that it will be nearly impossible for you to hit the ball offensively. When that happens, you may be able to blunt their edge by putting an unconventional serving strategy into use—the Australian formation.

The tactic calls for an unusual alignment created by positioning your partner on the same side of the center line as you are standing (see the sketch). That way, if the receiver tries a crosscourt shot, your partner will be able to volley the ball directly across the net at the opposing net player. And that player will have to have extremely quick reflexes to return your partner's volley with anything on it.

Your partner's position at the net will usually force the receiver to change his crosscourt tactics and go for the more difficult down-the-line shot. So after you serve the ball, you should cross over to that side of the court to cover the down-the-line return. To increase the effectiveness of the Australian formation, it's best if you serve from a spot close to the center mark.

DOUBLES: HOW TO BREAK SERVE

PLAN YOUR RETURN STRATEGY

To win in doubles, you must be able to break your opponent's serve. The odds in doubles generally favor the server so you'll win or lose depending on your ability to break serve. If you and your partner can hold serve consistently during a match, you'll need only one service break per set to cement a victory.

Unfortunately, many club-level doubles players have such a defensive attitude when they step to the baseline to receive serve that they virtually hand the match to their opponents. The importance of a well-thought-out service return strategy becomes apparent when you consider the pressure that's on you, the receiver. As you're watching the ball leave the server's racquet, you must simultaneously be aware of each of your opponents' positions, react to the speed and spin of the serve and, finally, concentrate on making the stroke and placing the ball in the opposite court.

That's an awful lot to think about in the second or two it takes for the ball to reach you. Obviously, a pre-planned strategy will eliminate a few of the split-second decisions you're faced with and allow you to focus your attention almost exclusively on the task at hand, returning the ball solidly. Of course, you must remain flexible enough to change those plans during a match if the server is frequently catching you off-guard.

PLAYING THE PERCENTAGES

WHERE TO STAND

When returning serve, you should assume a receiving position that allows you to cover your opponent's serving possibilities most efficiently. To determine what this position is with each of your opponents, you should carefully size up their serving tendencies as your match progresses to see if you can detect any patterns that you can exploit.

For most players, the best receiving position from which to start is just behind the baseline, near the corner of the singles court assuming that the server is hitting from midway between the center mark and singles sideline. From this position, you should be able to bisect a server's possible placements of serve. For the second serve, you can usually afford to move a couple of feet inside the baseline.

Once you get an idea of a server's capabilities, you should adjust your receiving position, taking into account the effectiveness of his serves and your own strengths and weaknesses. For example, if he hits most of his first serves to the deuce court down

the middle and you're a right-hander with a weak backhand, shift to the left slightly to invite him to hit to your stronger forehand side.

AIM THE BALL

The placement of your return should depend to a large degree on the mobility, aggressiveness and volleying skill of the server's partner at the net. Assuming that he's a good, club-level player who doesn't poach very often, your best option is a crosscourt return hit with medium pace to the feet of the onrushing server (A in the diagram) or one that's angled crosscourt into the alley (B).

The crosscourt return allows you to hit over the lower part of the net, making it a higher percentage shot. And by aiming at the server's feet, you put pressure on him or her and make it easier for you to join your partner at the net. You're trying to make the server hit the ball up with a half-volley or low volley; if all goes well, you or your partner can then move in on the ball and volley it down for a winner.

Angling a return into the alley is more difficult. It requires a lot of touch and control since the ball must land short to be effective. But when the shot's hit properly, the server has to charge in to reach the ball and

then hit up to clear the net. And since the shot has little pace on it, you'll have more time to reach your volleying position.

VARYING YOUR RETURNS

HOW TO FOIL A POACHER

By the end of the third or fourth game of a doubles match, the opposing teams have had a chance to feel out each others' strategies, strengths and weaknesses. That's usually the time when the server's netman begins to take liberties and poach on your crosscourt returns.

To counteract that, it's a good idea for you occasionally to hit a return down the line even earlier in a match to try to catch him starting crosscourt to poach (see diagram). Your return may not win the point—particularly if the netman has held his position at the net. But at least it serves notice to him that he'd better defend his alley and be more selective on his poaching attempts.

Generally, a down-the-line return will be most effective when the serve is delivered to the corner of either service court. This placement opens up a better angle for you to work with. Serves down the middle force you to hit directly toward the netman if you try to go down the alley, and that drastically reduces your chances for success. If he's a decent player,

he should be able to put the ball away promptly if your return is rising as it clears the net.

USE THE LOB RETURN

Sooner or later in doubles play, you'll come up against a server who's having a hot streak, hitting serves with deceptive spin and giving his partner at the net a feast of weak, floating returns that he can pick off like flies.

How do you break a pattern like that? The solution is to lob to return serve.

It's foolish for you to try to do something with a tough serve by slamming it back or going for a precise placement. Why not hit a high, defensive lob (A in the diagram) over the head of the opposing net-man to force him to retreat for the ball and to keep the server back, too?

And if you've spotted the server charging the net like a rampaging fullback on the previous points, try to lob over his head (B). He may not be able to reverse his momentum quickly enough to manage a good return. Don't forget, hit your lob high and deep to give yourself time to get into good defensive position.

You can use your offensive lob, too, on a weak serve or when the

other netman is crowding the net. Just be sure to hit the ball solidly, so that it will clear the netman's out-stretched racquet by a safe margin.

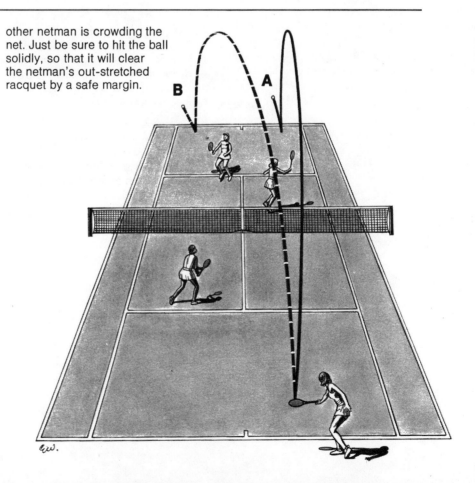

TAKING THE OFFENSIVE

LOOK FOR OPENINGS

In doubles, the server uses the forward momentum he generates in his service motion to help carry him

toward his volleying position at the net. You, as the receiver, don't enjoy that extra advantage. So you must rely on consistency and cunning placement of your shots to force short returns from your opponents that you can move in on.

In most cases, you'll find that you won't be able to advance to the forecourt as a direct result of your service returns. Against a good server, you'll have to create openings that will allow you to reach the net by probing the serving team's defenses patiently for weak spots. You can do that by varying the placement, speed and spin of your shots when your opponents are in volleying position.

However, if you face a weak server or are waiting for a second serve, you have a good chance to meet the ball early and hit a return that will put the server on the defensive. You can then continue forward and join your partner in the forecourt. Or, if you've hit an offensive lob that has cleared the netman, forcing him to scramble back toward his baseline, move to the net behind your shot.

HELP THE RECEIVER

When your partner is receiving serve, of course, you can't relax. Your role up at the net can be crucial. If you have good anticipation and the ability to put away any rising ball within reach as it crosses the net, it will make the receiver's job easier, allowing him or her to stay loose when returning the ball.

You should anticipate shots from your opponents by watching the

served ball land in the service court, adjusting your position slightly depending on where the serve is placed and determining which opposing player is going to hit the ball. For example, if the serve is deep into the corner, you should move a step to that side to better cover the court. As you're making this move, you should quickly glance at the opposing net player to see if he's moving to hit the ball. With experience, these things can be done in just a couple of seconds.

Also, get to know your partner's reactions to different types of serves because that will help you anticipate shots correctly. That knowledge is acquired in part by frequent communication, both verbal and through the use of hand signals, between the two of you during play.

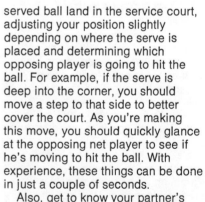

COORDINATING YOUR EFFORTS

MOVE TOGETHER

Many club players think of doubles as a game requiring lightning-fast reflexes and well-executed strategy. And that's right, except that they're neglecting probably the most important element necessary to good doubles play—a coordinated and practically instinctive way of moving together on the court with a partner in order to cover the most ground. When a doubles team fails to do that, wide gaps in court coverage are left open for opponents to exploit.

The key to moving well together with a partner in doubles is simple: just remember to play the percentages by edging over to the same side of the court where you or your partner have just hit the ball. For example, if you place a shot into the ad court, both you and your partner should take a step or two toward that side to cover your opponent's return (see diagram). This same shifting principle applies to forward and backward motion, too; advance together and retreat together.

Use this tandem rule even if you've never played with a particular partner

before and aren't acquainted with his or her style of play. It will help compensate for your unfamiliarity.

ATTACK THE SECOND SERVE

When an opponent in a doubles match fails to put his first serve into play, that's your signal to move a step or two closer to the net and think about returning his second

serve more aggressively. That's because your opponent will probably take pace off the serve by adding some spin to make the ball clear the net safely.

Against an experienced server, especially on a slow court, you can bet that most of his second serves will be kicking, twist deliveries down the middle. If you stay back at your baseline, you'll be forced to hit the ball above shoulder level—a difficult shot to return solidly. So it's to your advantage to get in as close as you dare and meet the serve early, while the ball's on the rise and before the spin has time to take full effect.

There are two places it's best to aim the ball. You can angle a shot short into the alley (A in the diagram) to force the server wide and open a gap between him and his partner or you can hit the ball hard at his feet (B) to make him volley up. Another option if you've been handling his second serves well is to hit the ball low and down the middle to reduce the angles of return.

DOUBLES: HOW TO SCORE AT THE NET

What's the key to winning at doubles? It's gaining—and maintaining—control of the net. That's because most points in a doubles match are won up there.

The team that's able to take command consistently at the net can dominate the match. They have the other team on the defensive—and often on the run. They can volley aggressively to set up points and then drive home winners off their opponents' weak returns.

So there's a lot more involved in playing the net than an ability to exchange rapid-fire volleys with the opposition. It requires an understanding of tactics and good coordination between partners.

The partners usually work best together when their styles of play complement each other. On most of the more successful doubles teams, for example, you'll notice that one member is often a steady player who possesses good touch and control, and who sets up points with deft placements. The other member is a shotmaker who's capable of finishing off points decisively with the big shot.

DOUBLES: HOW TO SCORE AT THE NET

GETTING IN THE BEST POSITION

WHERE TO STAND

Whether your partner is serving or waiting to return serve, you must be sure to position yourself properly at the net. You've got to be alert and ready to react to any shot from your opponents.

So when your teammate is receiving serve, you should assume a position that permits you to defend your half of the court well. Stand inside the service line, halfway between the center line and singles sideline (Player A in the sketch). Don't become rooted to that position, though. When you see that your partner's return will clear the opposing netman, move quickly toward the net so that you can attack.

When your partner is serving, you can afford to take a more offensive position, a step or two nearer the net (B). That should put you within one stride of reaching most returns (except lobs) hit to your side.

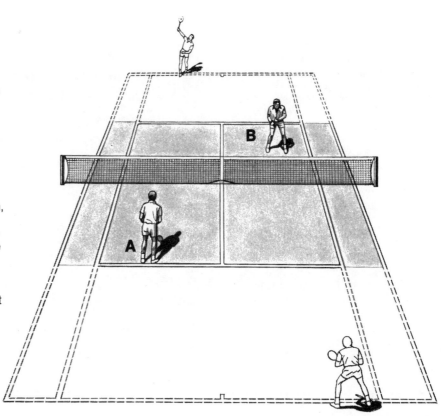

DEFEND THE CENTER

When you and your partner are in your volleying positions, it's physically impossible for you to protect the entire width of the net. Inexperienced doubles players, nonetheless, will still try to do that by standing too far apart at the net in order to cover the alleys—especially after they've been passed once or twice by shots down the line. But in doing that, they're opening up the center of the court for their opponents. And that's precisely the area where most volleys are hit in doubles—since the net is lowest there and the margin of safety is, thus, greater. So rather than becoming preoccupied with guarding against those occasional winners down the line, play the percentages and concentrate on defending the center (see sketch).

TAKING COMMAND AT THE NET

SET UP YOUR WINNERS

Satisfying though outright winners are in doubles, it's important for you to realize that the majority of them are the end result of a series of wisely-placed shots. They've been designed to pull opponents out of position and force weak returns. It's rare that a clean winner will be hit without those set-up shots.

When all four players are at the net, the best way you can set up a point is to aim your volleys at the feet of the opposing players. That will force them to hit rising shots that you can attack.

If you have good touch, though, you might try to angle a volley short into the alley (see diagram). It will open a gap between your opponents that you can aim for if the opposing netman is able to return the ball.

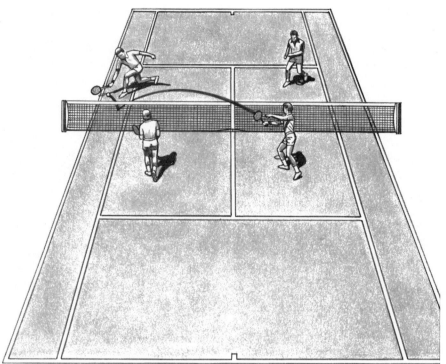

HIT DOWN WITH AUTHORITY

Once you've succeeded in setting up a point and forcing one of your opponents to send back a feeble return, you should be able to end the point quickly by hitting down on the ball with a hard, well-placed volley—as Billie Jean King demonstrates in the sketch (left).

As the ball rises over the net, focus your attention on it completely. Don't be distracted by the movements of your opponents across from you. Immediately after the ball is hit by an opponent, decide where you're going to place your shot. You have a number of good options—provided that you move in on the ball early and don't let it drop below the level of the net before you hit it. You can drive it down the middle, power it to the feet of your closest opponent or angle it hard toward the alley.

Every time you're able to hit down on a ball at the net, you have a good chance of volleying a winner. At the very least, your penetrating volleys should force weak returns.

GETTING AGGRESSIVE AT THE NET

USE THE POACH

One of the best ways to get an edge on an opposing doubles team, both physically and psychologically, is to poach effectively.

A classic poach is illustrated in the diagram: the server's netman anticipates a crosscourt return from the receiver, runs into the server's half of the court and picks off the return cleanly, hitting the ball down at the opponent's feet. Notice that the server, when he sees his partner poaching, moves in diagonally to cover the vacated half of the court.

If the poach is executed properly, the opposing netman will have trouble making a solid return. And psychologically, an attempted poach can intimidate an opponent.

PLAY SHOTS DOWN THE MIDDLE

There are few moments in doubles as frustrating as the time when you and your partner stage a painfully comic Alphonse-and-Gaston routine: a ball is returned down the middle within reach of both of you, yet momentarily paralyzed, you both let it pass cleanly between you for a winner.

Generally, you're expected to return all shots hit to your side of the court in doubles. But what about those shots hit down the center line? How should you deal with them?

If there's any confusion about which one of you is going to make the return, both of you should play the ball. After all, there's no time when you're at the net to shout "Yours!" at your partner and expect him to make a solid return.

It's often a good idea for a doubles team to agree before a match that shots down the center should usually be returned by the partner who can play the ball with a forehand. That's normally a club player's stronger side and, as a result, he can do more with the ball.

COPING WITH LOBS

CHASE THE DEEP ONES

To keep command of the net, you have to know how to retreat and return the lobs that your opponents will inevitably use to drive you back to your baseline.

You're responsible for running down and returning all lobs hit over your head into your half of the court. If an opponent hits a lob that's deep, you'll have to turn your back to the net in order to reach the ball (player A in the diagram). But you should look up and back over your shoulder to watch the trajectory of the ball.

When playing a deep defensive lob or an offensive lob, your partner (B) should retreat with you to the baseline. Remember, you must move together as a unit in doubles play.

SMASH THE SHORT ONES

When your opponents' lobs land short in your forecourt, it's important that you keep cool, even though you're eager to put the ball away. Basically, there are two places you should aim your overhead when a lob descends between your service line and the net. The highest percentage shot is to drive the ball directly between your opponents (A in the diagram). The other alternative is to angle your overhead toward one of the alleys (B), especially when the lob is extremely short. If you've just got an average overhead, though, and a lob lands at your baseline, don't always try to smash the ball. Your opponents may have come to the net behind the shot, and it could be tough for you to hit the ball past them. Instead, reply with a deep counter-lob to force them back.

HOW TO GET THE DROP ON AN OPPONENT

A NEW CHALLENGE

Does this sound like you? You have a respectable repertoire of consistent shots and a good grasp of strategy. You've reached a solid, intermediate plateau in your tennis development, but you're not satisfied with it. You have higher aspirations. You want more.

If that more or less describes you, then it's time for you to take on a new challenge: to master some of the more advanced strokes in order to add versatility to your style of play and to raise the level of your game to a new plateau. It will involve some sacrifice in terms of work on court. But if it's improvement you want, then practice is the only way you'll achieve it.

This chapter is the first of three dealing exclusively with advanced shots. On the next four pages, Billie Jean King and Vic Seixas demonstrate the basics of hitting the drop shot and the drop volley. Both are touch shots; that is, they require good racquet control and the subtle instinct of knowing just how softly to meet the ball so that it reaches its peak just over the net and then drops into the opponent's forecourt.

KEYS TO THE DROP SHOT

DISGUISE THE SHOT

The drop shot is a delicate stroke that puts underspin on the ball so that it clears the net and then falls short in your opponent's forecourt. It's the ultimate change of pace in tennis. Just like the baseball pitcher who occasionally uses his slow, change-of-pace pitch to cross up batters who are expecting fastballs, you can catch your opponents by surprise now and then by hitting drop shots off short balls during ground-stroke rallies.

But remember, you must be deceptive with the shot. You have to make your opponent wonder whether you're going to hit a deep approach or stroke a soft drop shot when you move in on a short return. The key to disguising your shot is to take a full backswing (above) just as you do on normal ground strokes.

MOVE INTO THE COURT

While you're taking your racquet back in preparation for the forward swing, you should be moving into the court, ready to intercept the short ball at the peak of its bounce. That should put you in a good, offensive position—well inside your baseline—where you can hit either an approach or a drop shot.

Use the drop shot, though, only when you're in front of your baseline. If you hit it when you're playing deep, your opponent will probably be able to scramble up and retrieve the shot. That's because the ball will take longer to travel the distance from your baseline to his forecourt.

Continue to disguise your drop shot even as you prepare to hit it. Step into the ball, swinging your racquet from high to low as you do for your slice ground strokes.

When I see a short ball coming to my backhand side (frame 1), I turn my shoulders and take my racquet back as I move into the court to intercept the shot (2 and 3). Notice that my backswing is full and that the racquet's *higher than the level of the approaching ball. That allows me to swing from high to low as I begin to transfer my weight forward during the stroke (4).*

CARESS THE BALL

Drop all pretense of deception just a fraction of a second before impact. At that point, you must open your racquet face slightly toward the sky. This subtle motion, combined with your descending swing, should allow you to gently caress the back and underside of the ball at contact, imparting the underspin that will make the ball die in your opponent's forecourt.

The stroke shouldn't be a hard, forceful one. You have to meet the ball delicately, almost with a feather-like touch, or else your shot will travel long and land within the retrieving range of your opponent. Imagine you're catching the ball on your racquet strings to develop a soft touch.

After contact, don't stop your racquet. Continue your descending swing.

FINISH THE STROKE

It's a common temptation with the drop shot to cut the stroke short, to chop it off immediately after contact with the ball. But remember that the drop shot, like your ground strokes, is incomplete without a follow-through.

You need to use a complete stroke to make sure that the ball will cross the net. A brief, chopping motion usually won't supply enough forward impetus to the ball.

Instead, you must keep the ball on your strings for as long as possible. Let your racquet continue out in the direction of the shot in a fluid, natural follow-through (above). And remember, because the drop shot is a low-percentage weapon, don't just stand there admiring your handiwork. If your shot goes too deep, your opponent may have time to move in and whack the ball past you. Always be ready for a return.

So far, my swing has been identical to that of a conventional ground stroke, disguising my intent from my opponent. Then, just before contact with the ball, I tilt the racquet face back slightly (5). I brush the bottom portion of the ball, imparting underspin and just enough forward momentum to get it safely over the net (6). Finally, I finish the stroke by following through naturally in the direction of the shot (7).

KEYS TO THE DROP VOLLEY

FOOL YOUR OPPONENTS

When you've taken control of play at the net and have your opponent pinned behind the baseline, it makes good strategic sense for you occasionally to surprise him with a drop volley, the net-player's version of the drop shot.

Like the drop shot, the drop volley is a tough, touch shot—especially since the ball reaches you much sooner when you're stationed at the net. And disguise plays an important role in hitting the drop volley, too. So your backswing should be minimal (above), a carbon copy, so to speak, of your preparation for a normal underspin volley with the racquet head above wrist level.

BRUSH THE BOTTOM OF THE BALL

Concentration and deft racquet control are two of the prerequisites for hitting a successful drop volley. You must be able to deceive your opponent with the shot, take the fast pace off the oncoming ball and then push it gently back across the net so that it drops and dies quickly.

The shot isn't easy, to be sure, but it can be developed with practice. The secret is to stroke downward and just slightly forward with your racquet. Just before impact, tilt the racquet face back a little as you do for a drop shot. Then, brush the lower half of the ball to impart underspin.

At this point, try to absorb some of the ball's speed by letting the racquet head give slightly. Then push the ball gently, but with enough forward momentum, to clear the net by a safe margin (above). Be sure to keep your eyes on the ball at all times and don't look up until you've hit the shot.

The key to hitting a successful drop volley is a compact backswing, just like the one you use for your regular volleys. In this sequence, I get a quick jump on my opponent's shot (frames 1 through 3) and assume a good position near the net with my racquet back and ready. From this position, I can hit either a drop volley or a deep volley. Notice that my eyes always stay riveted to the ball (4).

Drop Shot/Checklist
1. Watch the ball.
2. Disguise the stroke with early preparation and a full backswing.
3. Swing forward from high to low.
4. Tilt your racquet face back at impact.
5. Caress the back of the ball.
6. Follow through naturally.

KEEP THE FOLLOW-THROUGH SHORT

Remember the natural follow-through you used to hit your drop shot? Forget it on the drop volley. Because you're so close to the net, you really don't need the momentum and direction that a complete follow-through gives you. Nor do you have the time to finish such a long stroke. You must recover as quickly as possible in case your opponent somehow manages to reach the ball.

So the follow-through on the drop volley should be brief and quick, like it is on your conventional underspin volleys. But there's a big difference: you don't punch through the ball in the direction of the shot. Instead, continue your descending stroke until your racquet finishes below the point of impact (above). This finishing position is practically a guarantee that you've brushed under the ball and not blocked it back solidly. And that means, of course, that your opponent will have to do some fancy scrambling to get to the shot.

Drop Volley/Checklist
1. Concentrate on the ball.
2. Take a short backswing.
3. Use a compact, descending stroke.
4. Brush under the lower half of the ball.
5. Finish with a short follow-through.

Next, I start my racquet downward and slightly forward (5) in the same kind of descending stroking motion that I would use to hit a drop shot. And at contact, I tilt the racquet face back a bit (6) so that these two motions will combine to brush the lower portion of the ball and put underspin on it. You can see, too, that my follow-through is very brief with my racquet finishing below the point of contact (7 and 8).

HOW TO SHORE UP YOUR NET ATTACK

ADD TO YOUR VOLLEYING ARSENAL

You've mastered the fundamentals of net play so that you're comfortable up there. You can crack off a conventional volley with some authority and your overhead is reliable enough to get the job done when an opponent tries to lob over you.

But do you know how to handle a high, rising shot above shoulder level? Are you equipped to deal with an opponent who likes to mix it up with you in close-range exchanges of volleys at the net? And can you cope when an opponent sends a drive screaming at your belly button?

These situations call for some sophisticated racquet work. And on the next four pages Stan Smith shows the technique you can use to pick off rising shots and put them away with high volleys, Julie Anthony offers a lesson in the lob volley, a useful weapon for terminating those rapid-fire duels at the net and Roy Emerson demonstrates the way to return hard drives that are aimed right at you with the reflex volley.

KEYS TO THE HIGH VOLLEY

PREPARE CALMLY AND QUICKLY

The high volley is a putaway shot, almost as deadly as a well-executed overhead. Why? Because the shot is usually hit off a weak, rising return from an opponent. The fact that you're close to the net and can meet the ball at shoulder level or higher means you have a large area of court to hit into with your racquet. You don't have to concern yourself so much with arcing the ball to clear the net; instead, you want to drive it, with plenty of pace and depth, in a nearly flat line into the other court.

The stroking motion of the high volley is quite simple. What can be tough is remaining patient while reaching quickly with your feet and racquet. Sensing a kill, many club players become over anxious on their high volleys and belt ball after ball into the net. So when your opponent hits a high shot toward you, prepare early and calmly. Move in for the ball, turn sideways to its line of flight and take your racquet up and back smoothly (see above). Above all, don't think that the point is won before you've even hit the ball.

TAKE A LONGER BACKSWING

On a conventional volley, you have to keep your backswing short (the racquet should go back no farther than your rear shoulder) because the ball arrives so quickly. But since you'll usually have more time to prepare to hit a high volley and since you're hitting down into the other court, you can afford to take a slightly longer backswing.

In the photo above and the high-speed sequence at the bottom of the page, you can see that I bring my racquet head behind the imaginary plane of my right shoulder on the backswing. Notice, though, that the backswing is still much, much shorter than the one I'd use to hit a ground stroke. And, of course, it's made higher above the court surface, at the level of the approaching ball.

After taking this type of a backswing, you'll find you can generate greater racquet-head speed during your forward swing. That, combined with good weight transfer into the shot, will put extra power behind your putaway volleys.

Early racquet preparation is a key element if you want to put away high volleys consistently. In the sequence above, I react immediately to my opponent's shot by turning sideways to the ball's line of flight (frame 1). Meanwhile, I use small steps (2 and 3) to adjust my *position so that I can stride comfortably into the shot when the ball comes into range. After taking a fairly compact backswing, I begin my forward stroke and weight transfer (4).*

HIT THROUGH THE BALL

You've probably noticed in the photo sequence below that the forward swing on the high volley appears to be a simple, uncomplicated motion. And it is, because you don't have to impart any kind of spin to the ball.

A gradually descending stroke, in which you hit the ball flat toward your target area, is all you need to put away high volleys. After all, there's no need for you to make the shot more difficult than it actually is by introducing the variable of spin to your stroking motion.

Instead, concentrate on meeting the ball squarely while transferring your weight forward. Keep your wrist and grip firm throughout the stroke and don't be tempted to swat at the ball in your eagerness to end a point. Hit through the ball just as you would on a ground stroke. The pace and placement of your high volley, not the ball's spin, will make the shot a winner.

FOLLOW THROUGH FULLY

The velocity of a high volley is not as important as your ability to place it in an area of the court where your opponent can't make a solid return. And the key to guiding the ball to that spot is to finish the stroke with a complete, natural follow-through. A prematurely shortened stroke will rob your volley of both accuracy and pace, giving your opponent a better chance to reach the ball.

Your follow-through should be a smooth continuation of the momentum you generated with your forward swing and weight transfer. After you've made contact with the ball, let the momentum take the racquet head well out in front of you in the direction of the shot (see above). Your weight transfer, when completed, should center most of your weight on your front foot. From this position, you should be able to recover quickly in case your opponent manages to make a return. But the chances of that are slim if you've placed your volley in an area of open court away from him.

It's not necessary to put a lot of spin on the ball when making a high volley. I swing the racquet forward on a gently descending path and hit the ball flat, making contact well in front of my body (5) to generate some power.

Accelerating the racquet head through impact insures a fluid swing and a solid shot (6 and 7). I finish the stroke with a natural follow-through that helps to guide the shot and complete my weight transfer (8).

KEYS TO THE LOB VOLLEY

SURPRISE AN OPPONENT

How do you return a low volley hit by your opponent when both of you are at the net? Because you're forced to hit up to make the ball clear the net, your best bet usually is to try hitting a well-placed volley at his feet to turn the tables on him. But there's another weapon you can use—the lob volley—and it may be just the shot to make your opponent think twice about crowding the net again. You can even use the stroke occasionally to catch him in mid-stride as he runs in behind a return.

The lob volley is a touch shot that's designed to surprise your opponent by sending the ball sailing over his head and into the backcourt. It's a low percentage shot, though, so you're better off picking off balls above net level with conventional volleys. Prepare to hit the lob volley just as you would to hit a normal volley. Quickly turn sideways to the ball, pivoting your shoulders to take your racquet back. Flex your body to get down to the level of the ball (see above).

DISGUISE THE SHOT

When you hit a drop shot or drop volley, the effectiveness of the stroke depends on your ability to disguise the shot through contact with the ball. The same goes for the lob volley. Your preparation and backswing should be identical to what you'd use for a regular volley.

The difference occurs a fraction of a second before impact—when you tilt the racquet face back a bit toward the sky. Sounds familiar, doesn't it? That's exactly what you do to hit a drop volley off a low return. For the lob volley, though, you should make solid contact with the ball instead of brushing under it to impart underspin, and lift the ball into the air (see above) by moving your racquet on a smooth rising plane.

Try to practice hitting the ball firmly enough to clear your opponent and his racquet, yet not send it out of bounds beyond the baseline. A good guideline is to hit your lob volley no harder than you would a conventional low volley. That amount of force should give the ball enough lift and depth to send your opponent scrambling back toward his baseline.

KEEP YOUR FOLLOW-THROUGH FLUID

An abrupt finish to your stroke is usually an invitation to disaster: the ball will pop off your strings with little or no control, setting up your opponent for an easy overhead smash. A choppy stroke might also send the ball long.

For your safety at the net (you don't want to face an opponent's overhead at close range) and success with the shot, be sure to end your stroke with a fluid follow-through. After impact, keep your racquet head moving upward on a gradually rising path so that it follows the direction of the departing ball (as I'm doing in the photo above).

You can see that my follow-through isn't overly long, but it's sufficient to help me guide the ball. Once you've completed your stroke, get back into volleying position quickly. Even if your lob volley isn't a clean winner, you'll probably still be able to close out the point on the following shot because it will be difficult for your opponent to make a strong return while running down your lob.

This shot calls for a simple, compact stroke. At left, you can see that my first move (frames 1 and 2) is to pivot to my forehand side, start toward the ball and begin bending down. My backswing is very short (3) and, at contact, I tilt the racquet face back slightly toward the sky (4).

I move the racquet head up smoothly through contact to lift the ball high enough to clear my opponent at the net (5). And my follow-through is fluid (6) for maximum control of the shot.

KEYS TO THE REFLEX VOLLEY

SELF-DEFENSE

Have you ever found yourself cringing at the net when a blistering drive heads straight for your hip? What you learn quickly enough is that worrying doesn't slow the ball down. You must react coolly and decisively in the split-second available, blocking the ball back across the net with a simple reflex volley to keep the point going.

It's a defensive backhand shot. You can't adequately protect your body, particularly your hips and stomach, with a forehand. The backhand reflex volley allows you to bring the racquet head quickly across your body in a simple and efficient blocking motion.

You can get a start on developing a good reflex volley by having your practice partner hit soft shots directly at your body. Then, have him gradually increase the pace until you get used to handling hard drives. Advanced players know an opponent's racquet-side hip is a vulnerable target. And you can bet they'll aim for it frequently in a match!

Fast reactions are demanded for the reflex volley. From my ready position (frame 1), I use my backhand to block a sharp return hit directly at my hip. I bring the racquet head swiftly across my body to intercept the ball (2) and finish the stroke quickly (3) so I can get back into good volleying position.

Reflex Volley/ Checklist

1. Take the ball on your backhand side.
2. Bring the racquet head quickly across your body to meet the ball.
3. With a firm wrist, block and push the ball across the net.
4. Recover quickly.

HOW TO PUT THE FINISHING TOUCHES ON YOUR GAME

MAINTAINING AN OFFENSIVE EDGE

When your opponent is at the net gobbling up your attempted passing shots, do you yearn for a way to zap him? And when you're rushing the net, do you cringe every time your opponent laces a shot straight at your feet?

If you're a reasonably accomplished player, there are shots you can develop to deal with these situations: the topspin lob and the half volley. They're not easy and they take work to master. But they'll help you escape from some awkward situations on the court.

The topspin lob is a touch shot that's designed to be a clean winner. You've got to impart enough lift and topspin to the ball so that it arcs safely over your net-hugging opponent, bounces and then accelerates sharply toward the back fence.

The half volley, on the other hand, is a demanding shot you're forced to hit off a sharp return at your feet, usually when you're on your way to the net. You have to get down to the ball, meet it immediately after the bounce and send it back deep so you can resume your trip to the net.

KEYS TO THE TOPSPIN LOB

WATCH FOR THE RIGHT OPPORTUNITY

Where's your opponent on the court? That's the first consideration you should take into account before attempting the advanced topspin lob. If he's crowding the net and showing no respect for your passing shots, then it's a good time for you to spring the topspin lob on him and force him to think twice about playing you so aggressively in his forecourt.

If you're in good position near your baseline, begin the stroke by taking a full backswing as you move to intercept the ball (see above). Your opponent will probably expect another passing shot attempt and be caught off guard by your lob. Don't try the shot from too far behind your baseline, though, or he may have time to run the ball down and make a return.

TAKE A LOOPING SWING

The amount of topspin you put on the ball, coupled with the depth of the shot, will largely determine how successful you are with your topspin lob. It's that rapid forward rotation of the ball that makes it drop sharply into your opponent's court and then kick abruptly away from him as he runs toward his own baseline.

To get that kind of heavy topspin on your lob, you have to take a hard, looping swing at the ball. And that means you must drop your racquet head way below the line of flight of the approaching ball as you begin your forward swing (see above). Then with your wrist cocked, you can swing the racquet upward to make contact.

At first, it may be very difficult for you to convince yourself that such a swing won't send the ball over the fence. But you'll soon discover that the extreme topspin the swing produces will give you much more control.

When an opponent has been hugging the net for a while, I usually force him back with a topspin lob. I prepare for the shot just as I would for any normal ground stroke (frames 1 and 2). In fact, my opponent has no reason to *suspect anything but another attempted passing shot, judging by my racquet position (3). Then, I start my forward looping swing (4).*

SNAP YOUR WRIST FOR MORE SPIN

The moment of impact, of course, is the most critical point in your stroke. Because your swing is fairly vertical, you don't have much margin for error in meeting the ball.

Racquet-head speed is important, too, when you're trying to generate heavy topspin. To get your racquet head moving as past as possible, uncock and snap your wrist upward a fraction of a second before you strike the ball.

Remember, though, that the stroke is not simply a vertical flicking motion. Although that type of swing would produce a madly topspinning shot, the ball would not have enough forward momentum to clear your opponent. And he'd be able to slam it past you for a winner. Instead, hit forward and through the ball (see above) to give it the depth you need. Try to make contact with the ball out in front of your forward hip.

FINISH WITH A FULL FOLLOW-THROUGH

Your guarantee that you've hit through the ball completely —and imparted enough topspin and depth to the shot— is a high, full follow-through. Your racquet head should finish almost directly overhead (see above). In fact, once you've made contact with the ball, your upper body should open to face the net and you should be able to watch the shot over your racquet arm.

Now is not the time to stand flat-footed, admiring your lob. If it's short, your opponent will probably blast it back out of reach. However, if your lob safely clears your opponent's racquet, move in and take an offensive position at the net .

Where should you try to place your topspin lobs? Your safest bet is to direct them crosscourt, corner to corner. That will give you the greatest length of court to work with on the shot.

During my loop, notice that the racquet head is way below my wrist level (5), picking up momentum. From here, I can swing rapidly upward toward the ball so I'll be able to give it heavy topspin. Then, through impact,

I snap my wrist, too, to generate more racquet-head speed (6 and 7) and brush up the back of the ball. I complete the stroke with a high, full follow-through (8).

KEYS TO THE HALF VOLLEY

PREPARE INSTINCTIVELY

The half volley is to tennis what the sand trap shot is to golf. Both strokes often intimidate the average player to a point where he or she is unable to swing at the ball smoothly and properly. The result is usually a blown shot.

You should realize, though, that the half volley is a relatively simple and compact stroke mechanically. It's the timing and concentration required that make it a tough shot. So the key to hitting consistent half volleys is to develop quick but calm reactions by practicing the shot until it becomes almost instinctive.

The first step in executing a half volley is to prepare quickly by turning sideways to the approaching ball and taking a short backswing (see above).

LIFT THE BALL OVER THE NET

You should meet the ball just in front of your forward foot a fraction of a second after the ball bounces on the court. To eliminate a scooping type of swing, you have to get down to the ball so your racquet will be roughly parallel to the ground. You do that by flexing your body at the waist and bending your knees as you take your racquet back.

Bring your racquet forward on a gently rising path to meet the ball after it bounces. That should give the ball enough lift to clear the net safely. Hit the ball firmly with a steady wrist and keep the ball on your racquet face for as long as possible for maximum control (see above).

Don't try to hit the ball too hard; you want to use a controlled swing that will allow you to meet the ball solidly. Remember, your objective isn't to hit a clean winner; it's to return the ball deep so you can continue advancing to the net.

When an opponent's shot heads toward my feet as I move to the net, my first reaction is to turn sideways to the ball's line of flight and take a backswing (frames 1 and 2). At the same time, I bend my knees and flex my body (3) to get down to the level of the ball. Then, with my racquet almost parallel with the ground, I start my forward swing (4).

Topspin Lob/Checklist
1. Watch the ball carefully.
2. Use a looping swing from low to high.
3. Make contact with the ball out in front of your forward hip.
4. Snap your wrist at impact to generate racquet-head speed.
5. Follow through almost directly overhead.

FOLLOW THROUGH NATURALLY
My half volley stroke, as you can see in the high-speed photo sequence at the bottom of the page, is a compact and simple one. The total swing is a lot briefer than it is on my normal ground strokes. But my follow-through is just about as complete as possible—considering my low, half volley position. And yours should be, too.

A natural follow-through is important for the half volley because it means that you've hit through the ball completely. So let your racquet head continue forward in the direction of the shot (above) after impact. If you don't then you're likely to pop the ball off your strings with little control and provide your opponent with an easy sitter to wallop away.

Finally, keep in mind that the half volley is not something you should go out of your way to hit. Avoid the shot if you're able to move in close enough to volley the ball. And, if your opponent's shot isn't hit with too much pace, stop, back off a step and let the ball bounce. Then, hit a solid approach shot and continue toward the net.

Half Volley/Checklist
1. Concentrate intently on the approaching ball.
2. Prepare quickly with a compact backswing.
3. Flex your body and knees to get down to the shot and stay there through the stroke.
4. Move the racquet head forward smoothly to lift the ball over the net.
5. Let your racquet continue naturally in the direction of the shot.

I make contact with the ball (5) using a gently rising stroke. I swing firmly, but under control, so that I don't rush the shot. And my concentration on the ball never wavers. Notice that I stay down on the stroke even after impact (6). I let the racquet head continue to move away from my body in the same direction as my half volley (7 and 8) in a smooth and natural follow-through.

TACTICS FOR WINNING MATCHES

HOW TO PREPARE FOR A TOURNAMENT

Ready to give organized competition a try? It might be just the change of pace you've been looking for—particularly if you've been beating your friends fairly consistently in regular weekend matches.

More importantly, though, organized competition will offer you an excellent opportunity to improve your overall level of play. You'll be able to refine your strokes, experiment with strategies, face a variety of playing styles and learn how to deal with the pressures created by different match situations. In short, you'll become a more complete tennis player and have fun in the process.

There are a number of local events you can enter, many at your own club, that will give you a taste of tournament tennis, satisfy your competitive drive and sharpen your playing skills, all at the same time. The most common are challenge ladders and pyramids, league play, single-

elimination tournaments, consolation tournaments, double-elimination tournaments and round robins.

CHALLENGE LADDERS AND PYRAMIDS

Unlike most club-level competitions which last only a day or two, challenge ladders and pyramids provide an exciting means for you to compete with members of comparable playing ability on a continuous basis. The sought-after goal? To occupy the top position on the ranking ladder or pyramid, of course!

As their titles imply, challenge ladders are predicated on direct "challenges." Let's say, for example, that you're in the middle of a ladder. Although rules vary from club to club, you're usually allowed to challenge one of the two players directly above you. Win and you move up into his position. He must then step down a "rung." If you lose, though, you return to your previous position, and no changes occur in the ladder rankings.

Challenge pyramids operate on the same basic principle, except that challenging is done by "levels" (you

can play one of a group of players on the level above you) rather than by rungs. Use of this system allows more members to participate and usually results in a more active shuffling of the rankings.

LEAGUE PLAY

If team competition is what you're looking for, then league play is for you! Within recent years, it has become the fastest growing type of competition in the sport.

The reason for its popularity is simple: league play introduces club players, whether beginning or advanced, young or old, to competition with players from other clubs or regions—people they wouldn't have met otherwise. The team aspect promotes friendship and competitive spirit, too, and that's especially important for juniors. It prepares them for the tournament scene by exposing them to travel, new surroundings and unknown opponents.

What's league play like? Typically,

each interclub contest consists of five matches: two singles, two doubles and one mixed doubles. It's up to your pro to decide which matches you'll play (usually, you're allowed to complete in only two). Each match victory is worth one point to a team. So unlike most tennis competitions, you're not simply playing for yourself.

SINGLE-ELIMINATION TOURNAMENTS

Are you the type of player who enjoys doing battle with tough opponents? Who always seems to perform best in do-or-die situations?

If that sounds like you, you're likely to do well in single-elimination tournaments. That's because this type of tournament format presents you with the challenge of winning a series of must matches if you're to take the title. One loss and you're out. All entrants get their first-round pairings in a blind draw.

Whether you take home the first prize or lose in an early round, participation in such a tournament is a valuable learning experience. You quickly discover that you can't afford to let your thoughts wander beyond the match you're currently playing.

CONSOLATION TOURNAMENTS

When you lose in the opening round of a single-elimination tournament, don't start packing your tennis gear until you've found out if a consolation event is going to be played.

Some clubs stage these tournaments to give all first-round losers a second chance to compete for a prize and to compensate, to a degree, for their initial disappointment. In most cases, moreover, second-round losers in the main event are also allowed to play in the consolation tournament—provided that they had drawn byes in the first round.

The format of a consolation tournament is identical to that of the single-elimination tournament. The main thing to remember in playing a consolation tournament is to forget. That's right! Don't dwell on your loss in the first round of single elimination. You can't change the outcome. Just concentrate on your present match and prove that you really are a winner.

DOUBLE-ELIMINATION TOURNAMENTS

Have you ever had a bad day in a tournament, lost a match because you played far below your potential, and wished you had a second chance to redeem yourself and win the event?

You get that opportunity in double-elimination tournaments. That's because under the double-elimination format, a player must lose two matches to be knocked out of the event. So regardless of the round in which you lost, you still have a shot at the title.

Sounds great, doesn't it? Unfortunately, double-elimination tournaments are rarely held at the club level for a couple of good reasons. First, they best accommodate only a small number of contestants—eight usually, but 16 tops. And second, they're difficult to organize without the help of a sharp, experienced tournament director. If you've ever seen the draw sheets from the Grand Prix championships, for example, you'll understand. They can be confusing to follow since they seem to resemble complex chemical equations.

Give the double-elimination events a try, though, when your club does hold them. Take advantage of the two chances you've got to win a tournament.

ROUND-ROBIN EVENTS

For an exciting mix of competition and the opportunity to face a variety of opponents, few tournaments in tennis can rival a well-organized round robin.

How does it work? Let's assume that you've entered a round-robin tournament with seven other people. Put simply, over a period of time you'll get to play each of the other contestants in the group at least once. And the player with the best won-lost record after the cycle is completed is the winner.

There are variations, of course. For example, it's sometimes necessary to divide the players into two or more round-robin groups to accommodate a large turnout. After each group completes its schedule of matches, a playoff is held between the top finishers in the groups to determine the overall champion.

Because you're never really elimi-

nated in a round robin, you get to play a lot of tennis and make new friends. Even if you lose a couple of matches and know that you can't finish at the top of your group, you can still get plenty of enjoyment out of playing the role of a spoiler.

PREPARING FOR A TOURNAMENT

Your decision to enter any type of tennis competition should entail a commitment on your part—a desire and determination to get yourself in peak physical condition, to hone your strokes and to prepare mentally before the event begins. Frantic, eleventh-hour practice sessions and exercise routines usually detract from your performance on court by increasing tension and fatigue. So begin preparing a couple of weeks in advance to maximize your chances of success.

To get the most benefit out of tournament play, it's important for you to be in good shape. If you follow a sound exercise program throughout the year, you'll go out on the court for a match feeling stronger and, as a result, more confident. You'll be able to move quickly, but smoothly, to intercept your opponents' returns. And often, your top physical condition will be a major factor in helping you outlast a tough opponent.

Practice is essential, too. You can't win a tournament with shaky strokes and indecision, even if luck is on your side. It's in your routine practice sessions that you develop consistency in your strokes and the confidence in your game that's necessary for match play.

Finally, how many times do you think you've lost because you've gotten down on yourself during a match? Probably more times than you care to remember. That's why it's so important for you to have a good mental attitude going into a tournament. The ability to learn from your losses, to discover what went wrong and then correct it, is the mark of a good tennis player. That's the way to upgrade your game and to move toward fulfilling your potential in tennis.

HOW TO PREPARE FOR A MATCH

It's about one week before your first tournament and you think you've prepared well for the challenge. You've exercised religiously, practiced conscientiously and developed a positive mental attitude in getting ready for the upcoming event. Yet you seem to get a little more nervous each day as the match approaches. What more can you do?

Now is the time for you to begin your second phase of preparation—one that allows you to focus your attention exclusively on the first match and the opponent you must deal with, rather than on the tournament experience as a whole. Remember, you'll face only one opponent at a time during a tournament. Think in those terms.

Before you play in a tournament, try to establish and follow a pre-match routine that will allow you to channel your nervous energy into productive, confidence-building activities. Your routine should include working on your weaknesses, scouting your opponent, checking your equipment, eating healthy pre-match meals, psyching yourself up for play and, finally, warming up thoroughly.

Use the routine outlined here, along with any modifications you choose to make, as your checklist before you play a match. You should feel confident and fit as a result when you step onto the court for that first match.

WORK ON YOUR WEAKNESSES

The extent to which you're willing to go out on a court beforehand, work up a healthy sweat and work on your game will usually determine your success in tournaments. Even the pros spend a lot of time each day honing their strokes in order to raise the levels of their play.

Your goal in preparing for a tournament match, therefore, should be to try to shore up your weaknesses during practice sessions. Reduce the number of weak links in your game that an opponent can attack. For example, if you know your next

opponent has a strong serve-and-volley game and your passing shots leave a lot to be desired, plan your practice time to concentrate on those shots. Always remember your ultimate objective: to transform your weak strokes into strong ones.

In your zeal to correct your deficiencies, though, remember to continue practicing your strengths, too. You wouldn't want those strokes to become ineffective through disuse.

SCOUT YOUR OPPONENT

Like a military commander who uses reconnaissance reports to design his attack on an enemy, you can take a big advantage into a match if you've been able to scout your opponent beforehand and discover which shots make up his heavy artillery.

The best way to scout an opponent is to watch him while he's playing another match. From courtside you're under no pressure so you can carefully analyze his playing style. Ask yourself questions such as: how does he move for balls? What shots does he rely on during critical points? How often does he come in on his serve? Which shots give him the most trouble?

Whether you actually chart his tendencies or just get a general impression of his playing style, you'll be armed with valuable knowledge when you go into your match with him. Don't overdo this type of scouting, though. If your opponent's an excellent player, you might run the risk of subconsciously convincing yourself that you don't have a chance of beating him.

You can do some scouting on the court, too, in your warm-up with an opponent. Try to test him with a variety of shot placements and spins to see how he handles his returns. And give him a few lobs so you can see his overheads. You could discover his Achilles heel—a weakness that you can attack during the match.

CHECK YOUR EQUIPMENT

A newcomer to tournament tennis is usually fairly easy to spot at an event. He's the one carrying a single racquet around the courts and clutching a racquet cover that contains his wallet, watch, some loose change and a comb. Not exactly prepared for on-court emergencies, is he?

That's why you need to use some foresight in choosing the equipment and supplies that you're going to bring to a match. Who knows when a string will pop in your racquet or when a shoelace will snap? You have to be prepared for such contingencies.

The night before a match, set aside the things you'll want at courtside: a spare racquet, shoelaces, towels, sweatbands, a visor, suntan lotion, sunglasses, Band-Aids, adhesive tape, an elastic bandage, a thermos of juice or water and anything else you think you might need. This thorough preparation will eliminate one more distraction you'd have to contend with on the day of your match.

EAT PROPERLY
BEFORE A MATCH

For years, athletes have sought a food supplement that they could consume before an event to increase their energy and stamina, thereby enhancing their performances. Recent trends have focused on megavitamins and even bee pollen!

But there's no substitute for a balanced diet. So far, medical science has shown that what you eat several hours before your match, especially the night before, has a more dramatic effect on your performance than the supplements currently available.

What should you eat the night before a match? A meal containing carbohydrates, such as a plate of spaghetti, a few pieces of bread and even eight ounces of beer, is ideal provided you watch the calories. These foods provide glycogen which your body needs to produce energy.

On the day of your match, eat a light meal about four hours, and never less than two, before you're scheduled to play to be sure that it will be completely digested when you step on the court. Avoid a big meal and stay away from greasy foods because they're slow to digest.

Fluids are important, too. Before you play, drink about eight ounces of water and, if it's especially hot and humid, sip a few ounces between games to avoid dehydration.

about five minutes on court to rally with your opponent before a match. And that's insufficient time to prepare your body for the running, twisting and jumping demands of the sport.

You might even like to work out lightly for about 15 minutes or so on a practice court, if one's available before your match, to work up a sweat.

Loosening up in the locker room and on a practice court will allow you to take full advantage of your pre-match rally. Don't go for winners in the warm-up; instead, try to groove your strokes. Move the ball around and hit with different spins to establish a stroking rhythm. Focus your concentration on the ball. Then, when the umpire says "Play!" you'll be ready to perform at peak efficiency.

PSYCH YOURSELF UP
If you watch professional tennis on television, you've surely seen some post-match interviews with the losing players. What's the one phrase that often surfaces in their comments? Probably something like, "I just had trouble psyching myself up for the match."

The "psyching up" that players refer to is the mental preparation that's so important before playing a match. Consider, for example, a situation in which you draw the tournament's No. 1 seed as your first opponent. Many inexperienced players would subconsciously hand the match to the top seed right then and there.

But if you're a smart player, even though average in talent, you should recognize the fact that you're the underdog, go out on the court feeling loose and play your own game, figuring you have nothing to lose. At the very least, you'll give the No. 1 seed more problems than you would if you're worrying about how badly he's about to beat you.

Conversely, if you have to play someone who's a lot weaker than you, prepare yourself mentally so that you'll be able to maintain a high level of concentration throughout the match. Never take any opponent lightly! Psych yourself up to play relaxed, error-free tennis and you're bound to do well.

WARM UP THOROUGHLY
Want to warm up for a match like the pros? Then you should start in the locker room well before your match by doing plenty of stretching exercises to limber up your muscles.

Why exercise in there? At most tournaments, you'll only be given

LEARNING FROM THE PROS

In their years of playing big matches in the world's biggest tournaments, the seven members of the TENNIS Magazine Instruction Advisory Board have had to develop strategies to meet every kind of challenge on the court. So for this special section, the editors asked them to recall especially formidable challenges they've confronted during their careers and the strategies they created to overcome them.

It's unlikely, to be sure, that you are going to face a match point at Wimbledon or the pressure of a critical international team competition—as the members of the Advisory Board have. But the same kinds of crises and tensions arise at every level of the game, whether you're playing in a major championship or a club tournament. It's all a matter of degree.

So this section is presented, not only for the fascinating insights it provides into the world-class game, but also for the important lessons that all serious players can draw from each of the experiences cited by the members of the TENNIS Magazine Advisory Board.

SEVEN WINNING STRATEGIES

VIC SEIXAS:
"I WENT CROSSCOURT TO STUN ROSEWALL"
SCENE: 1954 Davis Cup Final, U.S. vs. Australia, Sydney.

"It was a pressure-packed situation. My U.S. teammates and I were trying to avenge three straight defeats at the hands of the Aussies in Davis Cup finals. And to top it off, we were playing in Australia before 25,600 obviously partisan fans.

Tony Trabert came through with a win over Lew Hoad to begin the competition and the next match pitted me against Ken Rosewall. This was the one contest the Australians thought they had a lock on because of my poor record against Rosewall in '54. I knew exactly how he would play me: hit to my backhand and cover down the line. That's the way everyone attacked me because my backhand passing shots down the line were strong while my crosscourt attempts were relatively weak.

We had one heck of a rally on the first point, considering that both of us were a little tight. Then, sure enough, Rosewall came in behind an approach shot to my backhand and waited for my return to come down the line. I crossed him up, though, and sent my backhand crosscourt for a winner!

He had to respect that shot the rest of the way and it gave me enough confidence to help me take the match 8-6, 6-8, 6-4, 6-3, one of the most gratifying wins in my career. We eventually captured the Davis Cup 3-2.

To keep your opponents honest, try using one of your weaker strokes early in a match. If it's good, you'll give your confidence a shot in the arm. But even if you miss, you've served notice that you're not afraid to use the stroke during play—a fact that your opponent can't afford to ignore."

STAN SMITH:
"I BEGAN HITTING OUT TO DEFEAT NASTASE"
SCENE: 1972 Men's Final, Wimbledon.

"One trap that all tennis players fall into occasionally—regardless of their playing abilities—is that they think too much during a match.

I did just that in 1972 when I was playing Ilie Nastase in the final round at Wimbledon and it nearly cost me the title. We split the first four sets and I managed to go ahead 6-5 in the fifth. All I had to do was break Nasty and the Wimbledon championship was mine. But I started thinking too far ahead, anticipating the victory and not concentrating on each point. As a result, he took a quick 40-love lead and I thought: 'That's it for this game. Now, I'll have to hold serve at 6-all and then break his serve to take the match.'

Disgusted, I decided to hit all-out on the next point and not try to oversteer the ball. He served to my forehand and I knocked it off for a winner as he came to the net. Suddenly, it was 40-15. I felt better and I concentrated on hitting out instinctively. It paid off as I took the next two points with hard-hit backhand crosscourt passing shots. And Nasty finally crumbled at match point, netting a backhand overhead.

The final score was 4-6, 6-3, 6-3, 4-6, 7-5. So when you're in a tight situation on the court, forget about the score. Don't be overly cautious. Play each point as it comes and hit out confidently on your shots."

BILLIE JEAN KING:
"I USED MY SECOND SERVE TO BEAT GOOLAGONG AT THE U.S. OPEN"
SCENE: 1974 Women's Final, U.S. Open, Forest Hills, N.Y.

"You've heard the expression, 'You're only as good as your second serve,' haven't you? My belief in that piece of tennis wisdom has helped carry me through many tough matches through the years.

In fact, it was a second serve late in the match that actually nailed down my win over Evonne Goolagong in the final to take the 1974 U.S. Open title 3-6, 6-3, 7-5.

The pivotal serve came when I was down 3-4 and love-30 in the third set. After missing with my first serve, I decided I'd go for it on the second—just hit the ball hard, deep and with as much spin as possible, right close to the center service line. Despite the pressure that was on me, I felt I had to hit a great serve then or the match would be all over.

You know what happened? The serve landed in the corner of the service box, exactly where I wanted it. The serve was a winner! I was psyched and closed out the match.

Don't get the wrong idea, though. I didn't stand at my baseline and just take a wild whack at the ball. I prepared myself mentally for the stroke. I imagined myself hitting the perfect serve and placing the ball precisely on target. I think I could have hit a dime with that serve.

So as you step up to the baseline, imagine yourself hitting a perfect delivery and then execute! If you imagine yourself double-faulting, you'll probably do it."

TONY TRABERT:
"I SET UP MY OPPONENT TO TAKE WIMBLEDON"
SCENE: 1955 Men's Final, Wimbledon.

"Good shot selection, of course, always plays a crucial role in the outcome of a tennis match, whether you're thoroughly dominating an opponent or slugging it out with him point for point.

At Wimbledon in 1955, for example, my ability to choose the right shots, and execute them well, paid off in winning the title without the loss of a single set. And that was most apparent at match point in the final against Kurt Nielsen of Denmark.

Nielsen was a tall, strong serve-and-volley player who liked to crowd the net. My ground strokes were quite strong that day and I mixed up my passing shots well to win the first two sets 6-3, 7-5 and run up a 5-1 lead in the third.

Needless to say, I felt confident and fully in command at match point. During the rally, he stroked an approach to my backhand and charged the net. Although I was in good position to attempt another passing shot, I fooled him by rolling a crosscourt offensive lob out of his reach! I had been saving that shot for just the right opportunity.

Scout your opponent before a match to get a line on his or her tendencies. That way, you'll be better able to cope with a specific match situation."

JULIE ANTHONY:
"I SLOWED DOWN MY STROKES AND WON FAST"
SCENE: 1978 Avon Futures of Puerto Rico, San Juan.

"In March, 1978, I took home the biggest prize-money check of my career by winning the Avon Futures Championships. But the match that actually set up that title took place a month earler at the Futures event in Puerto Rico. I learned an important lesson there that you can benefit from, too.

My opponent in the quarterfinals was Sweden's Mimmi Wikstedt, a powerful serve-and-volleyer with a cannon for a forehand. She took the first set 6-4 but I was playing well. Mimmi was just playing better.

I was getting pulled into her style of play, trying to match her power stroke for stroke. I was digging myself a hole because she was thriving on the fast pace of my returns. Then, down a set and serving at 1-4, I hit a slow spin second serve that she hit way out of bounds. Then it dawned on me! I should take pace off the ball and hit safely down the center of the court since she's so grooved on my hard returns.

Using that strategy, I won that second set 6-4, taking five straight games, and I cruised through the final set 6-2. It helped me win the event, and later, the championships.

When you face an exceptionally strong player, don't try to play his or her game. Have the guts to experiment and change the pace of shots to throw off your opponent's timing."

ROY EMERSON:
"I HUNG IN THERE TO WIN IN THE DAVIS CUP"
SCENE: 1964 Davis Cup Interzone Final, Australia vs. Sweden, Bastad.

"Every one of you, I'm sure, has been in this type of situation before: you and your opponent are tied at one set all, but he's giving you trouble in the third, leads by a few games and is ready to serve for the match. Pretty disheartening, isn't it? If you stand there and think about it too much, you might just as well pack it in and head for the showers.

It's happened to me a number of times, once during a Davis Cup Interzone Final against Jan Erik Lundquist of Sweden. But my coach, Harry Hopman, told me to 'stay in there and keep firing away!'

I was down 5-3 in the fifth set and Lundquist had new balls to serve out the match. All he had to do was continue to play the way he had early in the set. But he became tentative, tried to play it safe on his ground strokes and netted a few serves.

Hopman and I sensed this defensiveness. So I went on the attack, taking the next four games and the match, 2-6, 4-6, 6-3, 6-2, 7-5. That ended Lundquist's string of 17 consecutive Davis Cup singles wins in Bastad and we went on to beat the Swedes 5-0.

Hop's advice is often the first thing that's forgotten when a player gets down on himself. So I'll say it again: don't give up until the last point is over!"

RON HOLMBERG:
"I UPSET LAVER BY NEUTRALIZING HIS STRATEGY"
SCENE: 1956 Juniors Final, Wimbledon.

"Sooner or later, you're bound to come up against a player who's convinced that a particular strategy will beat you. He's so determined, in fact, that he'll keep using that strategy—even though he's getting blown off the court because of it. He's the type of player you need to crack early. If you can neutralize his strategy, you'll destroy his confidence and pretty much sew up the match right there. An excellent example of that occurred when I was playing Rod Laver in the 1956 Wimbledon Juniors Final. Laver, of course, hadn't reached his prime yet and he seemed unwilling or unable to change his serving tactics against me in the match.

Laver knew that I had a strong return of serve, so his strategy was to serve into my body, hoping to handcuff me. Of course, it didn't take me long to recognize his game plan. I made sure I stayed on the balls of my feet, ready to move to either side quickly each time he served.

In other words, I didn't allow the ball to play me and it paid off in quite a few solid returns that caught him by surprise. I broke his serve the very first time and he never recovered. I breezed to a 6-1, 6-1 win.

As soon as you realize that an opponent is going to work on a certain element of your game, neutralize his strategy with well-planned shots of your own. If you crack him, he'll be putty in your hands."